PRINCE OF THE BLOOD

LOUIS PHILIPPE JOSEPH, FIFTH DUKE OF ORLEANS
Sir Joshua Reynolds, 1785

PRINCE OF THE BLOOD

BEING AN ACCOUNT OF THE ILLUSTRIOUS BIRTH, THE
STRANGE LIFE AND THE HORRIBLE DEATH OF LOUIS-PHILIPPE
JOSEPH, FIFTH DUKE OF ORLÉANS, BETTER REMEMBERED
AS PHILIPPE ÉGALITÉ, HERE SET DOWN FOR
THE FIRST TIME IN ENGLISH BY

EVARTS SEELYE
SCUDDER

COLLINS PUBLISHERS
FORTY-EIGHT PALL MALL LONDON
1937

THIS BOOK IS SET IN FONTANA, A NEW TYPE
FACE DESIGNED FOR THE EXCLUSIVE USE OF THE
HOUSE OF COLLINS, AND PRINTED BY THEM
IN GREAT BRITAIN

COLLINS CLEAR-TYPE PRESS : LONDON AND GLASGOW
COPYRIGHT 1937

Contents

5

CONTENTS

Illustrations

CHAPTER I

REVOLUTIONARY CRIMINAL TRIBUNAL

ESTABLISHED BY THE LAW OF MARCH 10TH, 1793, SECOND YEAR OF THE REPUBLIC

The Carpenter of the domain will make the necessary preparations for the execution of the Judgment rendered by the Tribunal against . . . ÉGALITÉ AND COUSTARD . . . condemned to the sentence of Death.

This execution will take place at four o'clock, in the Place de la Révolution to-day.

The Public Prosecutor
A. Q. FOUQUIER

At the Tribunal this 16th Brumaire
1793 ; Second year of the Republic.

Fouquier-Tinville, public prosecutor of the first Republic of France, scrawled in the names and the date, underlining them with wide black sweeps of his quill. The room was deserted except for his solitary figure seated at the wide table. Beside him lay his broad-brimmed hat crowned with black ostrich feathers, and under his right hand rose a pile of papers filled with the names and particulars of thousands of his fellow-citizens sentenced to appear before him and listen to the accusations which he was so well prepared to bring against them. His hand seemed to rest fondly upon these passports to death while his mind still lingered over the drama that had just been concluded in the empty room. It had not been a very big day, but still, a prince of the blood—once the idol of the streets, hated by his own class, fawned upon and despised by all the leaders, the weakest, the richest and the most notorious of all the great names in the greatest of revolutions, a member of the Convention and a regicide: one of that band who had laid the last stroke of the axe against fifteen centuries and fifty generations of the old régime.

Fouquier-Tinville smiled inwardly. A member of the Convention! He could hear even now the murmur of disgust and horror sweep through the great hall when the Citoyen Égalité, ci-devant Louis-Philippe Joseph, Duke of Orléans, had voted for the death of the King. They all came to bow before St. Guillotine in the end. Now she was about to kiss M. Égalité. And he had even asked her to hurry. Not many did that. When the judgment was read out by Herman, president of the Court, there had been the usual hush through the room. The trials were becoming rather casual but there was still something solemn, some thrill of power in the words that sent men, women, boys and girls to their death. Herman's voice was monotonous as he read:

"After the unanimous declaration of the jury, the Tribunal finding that Louis-Philippe Égalité, formerly Duke of Orléans, and Anne-Pierre Coustard, ex-deputies of the National Convention, are convicted of being the authors or complices of the conspiracy which has existed against the unity and indivisibility of the republic, against the liberty and security of the French people, condemns the aforementioned Égalité and Coustard to the sentence of death."

Philippe had been singularly indifferent while Herman was reading. No emotion whatever was visible on his heavy, florid face unless it were a contempt for the opinion of the Court. His tall, ponderous figure even had a certain dignity about it, as though the advantages he had enjoyed and trampled underfoot had asserted themselves at this fatal moment. He had turned to the Court when Herman had finished reading and said calmly: " Since you have decided to make me perish, you should at least have sought some more plausible pretexts to accomplish it: for you will never succeed in persuading any one whomsoever that you believe me guilty of all that you have declared me to be—and you least of all, you who know me so well," he continued, raising his voice slightly and turning to the foreman of the jury, Antonelle, a former marquis, and a former friend: " However, since my fate has been decided, I ask you not to let me languish here until to-morrow and to order that I be led to death immediately."

Fouquier-Tinville reflected that he had granted this wish, one of the few requests he had ever been called upon to grant to royalty. It would be fulfilled. He was one of those who had dug a trench around French history and filled it with corpses—all the past was sunk in quicklime, it could never come back—never, at least, while he was in control of the law. The division was made, the pulse was strong, the future was of his making, legally of course, with all the outward forms of a severe and savage virtue. There was a cold obstinacy on his thin, sinister face as he leaned over the long table in front of him to select the names of those to be condemned on the morrow. Yesterday's *Moniteur* lay on top of a heap of papers. He glanced idly at the back page. "*Spectacles*: Théâtre de l'Opéra Comique, rue Favart—All for Love, or Juliette and Romeo," he read. A slow smile broke the passionless detachment, which seemed to surround him with a menacing inhumanity. Sentimental drivel, he thought, echoes of the order of things which he had been appointed to stamp out. He turned back the pages of the *Moniteur* to Danton's speech in the Convention and began reflecting idly how the Tribunal would fare if it had such a man to deal with. Eloquence against ruthless purpose. Philippe Égalité had had neither eloquence nor purpose. It had been like dismissing into death the last shadow of a former scheme of things that had flourished in an immemorial past.

He gathered his papers together, rose, and according to his custom walked slowly downstairs to the court-yard of the Conciergerie to make certain that the tumbrels were ready.

. . . .

On April 13th, 1747, Louis-Philippe Joseph, fifth Duke of Orléans, of Valois, of Chartres, of Nemours, of Montpensier, prince of the blood, Chevalier of the Orders of the King, Colonel-in-Chief of the Huzzars and light troops, Governor of the Dauphiné, Admiral of France, etc. etc. etc. etc., was born.

The rustle of gold braid, the flutter and bother about the crib of the royal infant is almost audible. Rarely has a man been born in such splendour and died in such ignominy as Louis-Philippe Joseph, Duke of Orléans, of Valois, etc. etc. etc., renamed Égalité, and guillotined on November 6th, at four o'clock in the afternoon, by order of Fouquier-Tinville, ex-financier and former lawyer of the Royal High Court of Paris.

Yet he was the father of the last King of the French. He bore one of the most illustrious names in the history of the greatest monarchy that Europe has known. At various times in the crowded years of the Revolution he was the centre of liberal opposition, of vast plots imaginary and real, of hopes and disappointments, of furious rivalries and obscure intrigues. As late as October, 1792, five months before his death, the Duke of Liancourt, then an exile in England, told Fanny Burney d'Arblay that the Duke of Orléans was indisputably the primary cause of the long and dreadful anarchy of his country; and Liancourt made no scruple to say that if he met him in London he would instantly cane him. The denouncements and furious ejaculations are endless. Mirabeau declared that he wouldn't have him for his valet. Talleyrand called him the cesspool of the Revolution, one of many epithets from that fertile mind. Lafayette's despising took an active as well as a literary form: he had him exiled after the October riots. And most of his biographers have built up mountains of abuse and created a tradition that has surrounded him with all the wrongs and weaknesses, and none of the ideals and achievements of that convulsed period.

Yet a few sentences scrawled on a bit of paper deny all the accusations.

When he was in prison awaiting his trial he wrote: "I should be contented to see all those who have not approved of my conduct recognise that I have not had any of the faults that the world has supposed I had. I cherish no rancour against any one and I will always be grateful when I am well treated. If it is with frankness one can count on mine upon all occasions."

In spite of this seemingly ingenious confession the task of lifting his faults from him is hopeless; he is swamped in them, bogged forever in history, but even the bogged can be well treated at their own valuation. Certainly Talleyrand showed his customary shrewdness when he wrote: "I have thought that a picture of the life of the Duke of Orléans would give the features and the colour of the weak and transient reign of Louis XVI.; that it would set forth in tangible manner the laxity of public and private manners under that reign, as well as the degradation in the form of government and in the habits of the administration: that a work undertaken with this view would faithfully depict the character of an important period of French history." All of which is true. And you must remember that Talleyrand himself was one of the most willing frequenters of the society of the Palais Royal, and although (or was it because?) the private and public manners were lax, it was Talleyrand who remarked, that he " who was not living before 1789, knows nothing of the charm of living." Even Talleyrand's righteous stricture upon the degradation in the form of government and in the habits of the administration must cause a sigh when one remembers that the charming writer in his later life was Foreign Minister of France and that, notwithstanding his breadth of view and uncanny capacity for clear thinking, he sold state papers from the Foreign Office to the Emperor of Austria for a private gain of half a million and a promise of a refuge with the enemy of his country if France got too hot for him. He knew, if any one did, how a degraded form of government could function.

. . . .

Having achieved the distinction of being born it seems hardly necessary to follow Philippe Égalité through the first years of his life, beyond mentioning the fact that he lived in the château of St. Cloud, watched over by the elderly and respectable Maréchal de Rochambeau and fed by three wet nurses, besides being attended by five women and two valets. In spite of this excessive care there is nothing to show that he was not an amiable baby; there are no records of unusual performances, mythical or hereditary, from which portents of future character can be earnestly deduced. As far as is known, he never strangled snakes in his cradle like Hercules, nor beat his nurse like Mirabeau. At five years of age he passed from the hands of women into the hands of men. According to the custom of the time he was stripped stark naked and made to parade in front of his father, who was attended by doctors, and lords and ladies of his Court. After having been declared in writing to be male, healthy and unmarked, he was ordered by his father to be clothed in new garments and given into the keeping of a governor, M. Pons Saint Maurice, who was charged thereupon with his education and made responsible for his upbringing.

There is a story told that when he was nine years old, he noticed an old war-worn and slightly threadbare chevalier of Saint Louis at the receptions in the Palais Royal, where many of the more needy of the aristocracy were in the habit of gathering. This particular worthy was distinguished by the innocence of his expression and the simplicity of his self-indulgence which took the form of an inordinate love of bon-bons. The young duke conceived the idea of presenting the old man with a huge cornucopia stuffed with sweets under which he hid forty louis. The following day the chevalier, having eaten the sweets and discovered the gold pieces, returned with them to the palace, supposing that there had been a mistake. Naturally he was told that there was no mistake. It is not a very good story, but it appears to be true, and we can only hope that the chevalier spent the forty louis on a wilderness of bon-bons.

. . . .

Among all the forces obscure and manifest which go to form the character of a man none is more far-reaching in its effects or so little studied in its origin as heredity. Philippe Égalité came of a warlike and voluptuous race. The title of Duke of Orléans had been created by Philip VI. in the fourteenth century. The title had twice become extinct through lack of legitimate issue and each time it had been revived by the reigning monarch. In 1661, Louis XIV. had bestowed it on his brother Philip, who had taken as his duchess, Henrietta, the third sister of Charles II. of England. The title has existed uninterruptedly since that date. Philippe's great-grandfather, Philip II., Regent of France, is especially noteworthy. He was a distinguished soldier and fought at Stienkerk, Neerwinden and Namur. He commanded in Italy and in Spain. He married the legitimized daughter of Louis XIV., Mlle de Blois. His ambition led him to be suspected of aspiring to the throne of Spain. Because of this he fell into disfavour at Court and became the centre of the opposition to the great king. "He drank to excess, had several bastards, frequented the lowest company, cursed and swore from sunset to sunrise, indulged in disgusting talk and took care that the reports of his excesses were bruited about all over the town." He practised black magic and held seances at which the Devil was earnestly invoked to appear. People even said that he had murdered his cousin. Yet he was called to the bedside of the dying King Louis XIV., who kept him a considerable time in private conversation and as he dismissed him said, loud enough for all those around him to hear, "You are about to see one king in the tomb and another in the cradle. Never forget the memory of the one, nor the welfare of the other."

As President of the Council of Regency of the young

King Louis XV (aged five) he was the guiding power and the virtual governor of the Kingdom. In spite of conspiracies against him he kept control of his position until February 15th, 1723, when the new king attained his majority of thirteen years. He then ceased being Regent to become Prime Minister until his death from apoplexy eight months later. His enemies did their best to turn the boy king's favour from him but without any success whatever. Louis XV. loved his uncle, and in return Philippe was wise in his advice and affectionate in his manner. It is the most pleasing side of a character that was said to combine the traits of "a braggard and a coxcomb." His habits were corrupt, his mind was intelligent and sometimes brilliant and his tastes were luxurious. One more fact—for the Regent helps somewhat to give the tone, gone somewhat flat, of his great-great-grandson. He had been responsible for the policy which favoured an alliance with England, and through it of "a firm and genuine peace for which the world had been yearning,"—but which, besides being enormously unpopular, had immediately led to war with Spain.

The Regency, writes M. Gaxotte, is a record of misery, extravagance and folly.

.   .   .   .

The Regent's son, Philippe Égalité's grandfather was in contrast a pious, cultured and crochety man who had retired to private life after an intrigue of Cardinal Fleury had resulted in his dismissal from the position of Colonel-General of Infantry. In his retirement he occupied himself by translating the Psalms and the

18

epistles of St. Paul. Among the people he gained the reputation of being a saint, while at Court he was considered to be manifestly mad. He held the interesting and bizarre opinion that those whom one cared for did not die but merely disappeared from earth to reappear a short time afterwards. So convinced was he that he refused to admit the death of a lady he had loved, and continued to pay her a pension which was set aside against her reappearance. He also believed that his son was incapable of being a father and the appearance of two grandchildren failed to convince him. He persuaded himself that they had been purchased and introduced secretly into the house, and he refused to see them at any time or under any circumstances, except upon his deathbed, when he admitted the two children to his saintly presence and bestowed a curse upon his grandson aged five. Naturally this scene was used later by the royalists to prove that even the child of five carried the grim signs of regicide in his candid eyes which the saint detected with unerring truth.

He believed his daughter-in-law to be an even more unfortunate object of commiseration than his son. He lived until 1752, and until that date, according to custom, his grandson bore the title of Duke of Montpensier, his son that of Duc de Chartres. Thereafter Philippe Égalité became Duc de Chartres until 1785, when his father died and he assumed the title of Duke of Orléans.

His father, Philippe the Fat, had been born at Versailles on May 12th, 1725, and had distinguished

himself in the campaigns of 1742-44 during the war of
the Austrian Succession. But his indecisive and in-
curious nature and his love of good living destined him
to inactivity. He had a horror of application to anything serious, he loved gambling better than conversation and hunting better than either, in spite of
being enormously fat and often falling off his horse.

He had married as his duchess the young and
beautiful Louise-Henriette de Bourbon-Conti, and
Louise-Philippe Joseph had been the child of their
first passionate and unrestrained affection, so unrestrained, in fact, was the eagerness of their amorous
behaviour that the Duchesse de Tollard remarked that
they had at last discovered the method of making
marriage indecent. This more or less public honey-
moon did not last very long. Louise-Henriette had
been brought up in the strictest manners and the most
religious surroundings, and finding herself suddenly
freed of her family atmosphere and married to a man
who was timid (one of the wits of the day irreverently
remarked that if a statue were to be erected to him it
should be that of a horse with Philippe lying underneath), tolerant and not unpleasant, she plunged into a
whirl of pleasure as soon as the first transport of her
married state had passed. She had dark, flashing eyes
and a spirit that mocked and loved life, invited
adventure and laughed at scandal. Her memory and
her reputation are cluttered with stories that doubtless
are as much due to her own extravagant invention as
they are to truth. Her tongue was sharp and indiscriminate. Once when the question of her son's

legitimacy was being bandied about she laughed and said, "When you fall on a pile of thorns do you know which one has pricked you?" And during the Revolution and the Restauration the enemies of the Duke of Orléans seized every supposition, this one in particular, and made him into the son of a coachman, picturing his mother as returning to her palace at dawn reeking with the odour of the brothel. So grotesque did the gossip of the day become that it was said among the public that in order to recover her sexual powers after these debauches she used to plunge into a bath of human blood. "The children of beggars, kidnapped and murdered, were assuredly the source of these horrible baths."

Political hatred if not always edifying in its wild assertions is almost invariably picturesque.

She died of consumption in 1759, when Philippe was twelve years old, and her death, it was freely said at the time, was as much due to her debauchery as to her lungs—she was thirty-three. After her death large numbers of obscene limericks and verses written by her were discovered by her bed, which caused much amusement as they were thought to be more wittily indecent than those that a certain abbé had recently circulated. It was one of the lesser but not unusual pastimes of great ladies to kill the heaped boredom that they feared worse than death, scandal, or illegitimate children. In her *Histoire de ma Vie*, George Sand tells how at her grandmother's she found boxes full of couplets, madrigals and biting satires. "I burned some of them, so obscene that I would not dare read them through, and these written by abbés I have known in my infancy and by a Marquis of the best blood."

There was a striking family resemblance in all the Orléans line only interrupted by Philippe's saintly and cursing grandfather. Father to son, the same heavy figure, the same temperament, the same love of war and love of pleasure, and as often happened when they were prevented by the King from taking part in a world of action, the same debauchery, gout and apoplexy. With such a heritage Philippe Duc de Chartres grew under the tutelage of Monsieur Pons Saint Maurice.

CHAPTER II

A GREAT QUESTION

EVEN his enemies concede to the young duke a slight, graceful figure as a boy, which was in contrast to his heavy-jowled father, and in spite of Talleyrand's attempt to represent him as malicious and cold-hearted he appears to have been well liked and to have shown even at an early age a great love of animals and a natural grace to the people around him. In that medley of brilliance, squalor, ceremony and carnival that composed the *ancien régime*, the education of a young prince was left entirely to tutors and lackeys who were as interested in maintaining the etiquette of their positions as they were in instructing their pupil. M. de Pons Saint Maurice, the chief governor of the Duc de Chartres, was a gentleman of exquisite manners and profound ignorance, who took all forms of social etiquette with prodigious solemnity. He had made himself indispensable to the Duke of Orléans by his ability to organise the entertainments at St. Cloud and Villers-Cotterets and to perform in private theatricals. His performance of *Alceste* was superb. At his command were an under-governor and a private tutor and between them they managed never to let their pupil out of sight. Even at night the tutor, the first *valet de chambre*, and the *valet de chambre de garde* slept in the same room with the Duke and had to present a report to M. Pons each morning. These weighty documents are not available.

Besides the governors and the tutor there were four *valets de chambre*, a barber and a surgeon whose attentions surrounded the child. He was brought up in a world that considered that it had reached completeness—which in fact it had—a world which saw no particular reason why the monarchy of Louis XIV. and its customs, habits, privileges and pleasures should not endure forever — or practically forever. To describe a large part of Philippe's education would be to describe a magnificent wardrobe and give details that would be interesting to tailors. There is an almost unanimous opinion among those who were acquainted with his education that he learned nothing. There was no work, no application, and no study. He was full of curiosity and completely lacking in will-power. He seems to have shown some aptitude for mathematics and a certain shrewdness in judging his companions. He rode horseback extremely well and he was a good shot. The attentions to his figure and his health were only equalled by the neglect of his character.

But in the background of eighteenth century health there was always, even for the most indestructible of men, a lurking shadow—the scourge of smallpox. Few diseases have caused such widespread devastation or such loss of life. The epidemic at the beginning of the century (1715) had killed three dauphins. One after the other Louis XIV. had seen his son the Grand Dauphin and his two grandsons, the Duc de Bourgogne and the Duc de Berry, succumb to the plague.

The grandson, who succeeded in 1715 as Louis XV., died of it in horrible suffering in 1774. And the number of famous men of the Revolution—Mirabeau and Danton to name only two—who bore the hideous pox marks only indicates how fearful and widespread were its ravages. At the beginning of the century it was known that the Turks used some form of inoculation against the disease, and following the information contained in the letters of Lady Mary Wortley Montagu, the doctors in London and Geneva were carrying out their first experiments and those with successful records already enjoyed a wide reputation.

There was, of course, opposition to the practice, as there is invariably to any innovation no matter how useful or beneficial to mankind it may be. It was true that there was a certain risk involved, and when the Duke of Orléans determined to expose his son to the risks of "this dangerous and detestable invention" in order to make safe the future of his house there were deep discussions of religious import, knotty questions of legal right and scarcely any examination of medical evidence.[1]   However, the Duke wrote to Kerpatry in London, one of the most famous practitioners, asking him to perform the operation, and when for some unknown reason the letter remained unanswered, he wrote to Tronchin at Geneva, who was said to have inoculated more than twenty thousand persons and lost none. The Swiss doctor examined the young Duc

[1] In 1769 Horace Walpole wrote a description of a visit to the apartments of Mme de Maintenon at Versailles and added: "Oh, we went to the apothecaries, where they treated us with cordials and where one of the ladies told me that inoculation was a sin, as it was a voluntary detention from Mass and a voluntary cause of eating ' gras.'"

de Chartres and declared first of all that there was some danger of his becoming hunchbacked—a family heritage on his mother's side. To obviate this hideous and unfortunate ailment he hung the child on a door where he manipulated and stretched his limbs with apparent success. After this preliminary demonstration he inoculated him against smallpox with complete success, and became the rage in fashionable Paris where he accumulated a large fortune.

After this brief appearance before the world the Duc de Chartres is lost for years among "a crowd of embroidered, gilded, dressed-up, powdered little gentlemen decked with sword and sash, carrying the chapeau under the arm, bowing, presenting the hand, rehearsing fine attitudes before a mirror, repeating prepared compliments, pretty little puppets in which everything is the work of the tailor, the hairdresser, the preceptor and the dancing-master." He is not a hero, he is a background; and though his rank as prince of the blood made him a centre of form and ceremony, nothing in his personality indicated any sense of leadership.

In 1759, the year in which his mother died, he began his official life. During his first visit to Versailles he was received by the Dauphin and exercised a number of the prerogatives of his rank—for example he handed the King his shirt and he gave the Queen her serviette at dinner. These privileged duties he performed with no difficulty whatever.

We hear of him hunting with King Louis XV., of his appearance in the meeting of princes and peers presided over by his father, and finally, when he was nineteen years old, of his emancipation from M. Pons, his governor who remarked: "I have finished the education of a young prince who will make a noise, but he must not be offended—he does not pardon."

The "emancipation" of the Duc de Chartres in 1766 was an occasion for joy at the Palais Royal. Ever since his father had taken a new mistress nicknamed Marquise into his household there had been grumblings among the gay society. Philippe the Fat had chosen badly, they said. Marquise, whose real name was Etienne-Marie-Perrine Le Marquis, had carried as a girl, it was said, the flat basket of an oyster woman before she graduated from that humble employment to the Comédie Italienne, where her dancing had attracted Philippe to such a point that she danced her way into the princely bed and presented him with a natural son the following year and with twins the year after. The announcement of these events and the still slight odour of fish and oyster about the past of the new mistress visibly dampened the gaiety of the Palais Royal—especially as the Duke lived more and more in retirement at Bagnolet where he hunted and enjoyed a private theatre with Marquise, who defied etiquette, dressed like a man and took part in crapulous theatricals of the less interesting boudoir variety. The hold of this woman grew so strong over the Duke of Orléans that, as one commentator says, she succeeded in keeping away bad society as well as good and enjoyed the exclusive possession of her large conquest. So much, indeed, was this remarked that M. Pons Saint

27

Maurice, the high priest of decorum, was heard to murmur that the end of the House of Orléans was approaching if not already at hand.

For nine years Marquise had exercised her domination, until one day the ties of paternal affection overthrew the harpy in a manner that was in the best traditions of sentimental fiction. The young Duc de Chartres's appearance in society made it necessary for his father to entertain the world at Villers-Cotterets, and he found unexpected pleasure in the half-forgotten gaiety. There were many parties and the perpetual holiday that society awarded itself was more than usually brilliant. Universal carnival—music, dances and theatricals from morning until night and from night until morning, with many young and lovely ladies to take part in them. Philippe was enchanted— Marquise's tyranny seemed to be waning. But after the summer he returned once more to Bagnolet and comparative gloom settled over the mirth of Villers-Cotterets.

Then one clear October morning as he was preparing to leave for the day's hunting, his son suddenly appeared and declared that he wanted to join his father in the hunt. Philippe was much moved at this unwonted show of affection and the following day, reflecting on the fact that it was unseemly for his son to be in the company of Marquise who had gone hunting with them in trousers, he wrote her a terse note which terminated an intimacy of nine years. Among the inscrutable workings of sentimentality which are always worth recording even if they cannot be explained, this is one of the most fanciful. After formally announcing to his Court the arrival of three illegitimate children, Philippe dismissed their mother because she had been hunting in trousers with his legitimate heir. Moreover, this liberation from Marquise occurred at the very moment when his son was about to sow his extraordinarily abundant crop of wild oats. And to complete the picture Philippe thoughtfully chose a mistress for him in order to try to keep him out of worse trouble.

Anything rather than suffer from *ennui*. As the old woman said one day to Candide, "I should like to know which is worse, to be ravished a hundred times by negro pirates, to have one's rump gashed or to be switched by the Bulgarians, to be scourged or hung in an *auto de fé*, to be cut to pieces, to row in the galleys, to suffer any misery through which we have passed, or to sit still and do nothing?"

"That is a great question," said Candide.

CHAPTER III

MARRIAGE

"HE is a good-looking boy, well-behaved, not at all high hat and he could become some one worth while if you could get him interested in something and if you could get him away from the society of our imbecile bright young things." Although this was written about Biron by Mme du Deffand (whom Horace Walpole called his charming blind old woman) it might equally well have been written about Philippe about 1767. Armand Louis de Constant, Comte de Biron and later Duc de Lauzun, was the same age as Philippe. He was "courageous, romantic, generous and witty." His position was almost equally brilliant and he was the closest of Philippe's friends in the days after his "emancipation." Even later, when others turned away from him, Biron kept for him "the most tender feelings." He is indeed the only sympathetic character about Philippe at this time, and he seems by his charm to make up for the dreary debauchery of the rest.

Life was one wild party after another. But the Duc de Chartres, as Philippe was now called, was not, as his many enemies assume, a debauchee from the beginning, nor did he spend a large part of his time "listening to those inner neighings of a lascivious soul," as many people supposed. There was in fact

30

some cause for gossip at his reputed indifference to women and the worst was immediately assumed. However, his father in a burst of generosity which has a touch of farce about it supplied him with a young mistress, aged fifteen, named Rosalie Duthé. And as Philippe had been the source of Tronchin's fame and wealth, he now became the benefactor, as well as the lover, of Rosalie Duthé. His first mistress did not remain long with him but she managed her own affairs so well and with such *éclat* that she became one of the most luxurious and most sought after courtesans of the day. She had a vogue among the English roués, Lord Egremont was particularly fascinated. There is a glimpse of her later, "elegant and pretty," walking about one summer evening in the gardens of the Palais Royal with other women of light character; "for in those days no gentleman were ever seen with such people. If they joined them at the play it was always in covered boxes. Englishmen are less delicate on this point," wrote Mme Le Brun. "This same Mlle Duthé was often accompanied by an Englishman so devoted that, eighteen years after, I saw them still together at the theatre in London. The brother of this man was with them, and I was told that all three lived together. You have no idea, dear friend, what bad women were in those days. Mlle Duthé, for instance, spent millions; now that trade is nowhere, few would ruin themselves for such women." During the first days of the Revolution she retired discreetly across the Channel, having made as certain as possible that her financial affairs were in the hands of a trusted banker.

There is a curious collection of documents preserved in the Paris archives concerning the aristocratic
pub-crawling of the young duke. It is evident that he
was the follower rather than the leader of that incredible procession of rakes whose chief occupation
seemed to be to see how short and gay they could make
life without actually committing suicide. The police
officer, or detective, named Marais, who was detailed
to report on the royal pleasures appears to have been
overcome by boredom and punctiliousness. He
diligently records, for example, that at seven o'clock
on the evening of the twenty-seventh of February, 1769,
Philippe reposed in the arms of a certain Mlle Lavigne,
called Durancy, "*l'étoile de pensionnaire* at the house of
la Brissault." Other parties, more innocent and not
less inconsequential, are recorded by other pens. "On
one occasion," wrote a lady describing an evening
ending in Blind Man's Buff, "they upset the tables
and the furniture, they scattered twenty carafes of
water about the room. I finally got away at half-past
one wearied out, pelted with handkerchiefs, and leaving
Madame de Clarence hoarse, with her dress torn to
shreds, a scratch on her arm, and a bruise on her
forehead, but delighted that she had given such a gay
supper, and flattered with the idea of its being the talk
of the day."

Barrenness and artificiality are doubtless much the
same at any period, but never were they so absorbing,
so refined and so universal as at the closing of the old
régime. Everything must follow the fashion and there
was a fashion for everything. Once again it is George

Sand who wrote: "There was a certain way of walking, of sitting down, of saluting, of picking up a glove, of holding a fork, of tendering any article, in fine a complete mimicry which children had to be taught at a very early age in order that habits might become a second nature, and this conventionality formed so important an item in the life of men and women in aristocratic circles that the actors of the present day with all their skill are scarcely able to give us an idea of it." There was, in fact, a fashionable way of feeling or rather of not feeling, which an English traveller of the time, John Andrews, says carefully keeps at a distance every object that wears the least aspect of seriousness.

Philippe was soon attracted to a group of dé-bauchés, most of them, except Biron, older than himself, and there is an unedifying record of him swaggering in obscenity and trying to talk in a louder and more disgusting manner than his older cronies, a self-conscious and uncertain boy afraid of being laughed at by tarts, trollops, drabs and *viveurs*.

"To steady such a character," wrote the serious Marais, "one must hope that he may really fall in love with an honest woman who would have enough of a hold on him to make him adopt a more gentlemanly tone and stop using language that would make a carter blush."

But unhappily, the guide to his character at this period was not an honest woman, but a certain M. de Voyer, the oldest member of this intimate group. He was older than Philippe's father and had a great and unfortunate influence on the younger members. He had a considerable fortune and his talents as a talker had gained him a reputation. The younger men were impressed and flattered by his company. He talked the metaphysical jargon of the day. "It was always: The soul, space . . . the link of things . . . abstractedness . . . matter . . . indivisible, etc. etc." All these words, never explained, pronounced at intervals with gestures, reticent and mystic form, prepared the young adepts to believe. This shapeless rubbish of metaphysics, completely subjugated Philippe, and certainly explains a great deal in his character, though it may be doubted whether Talleyrand is right in saying that it accounts for his entire life. The fundamental principle of M. de Voyer's doctrine was simple. He denied the existence of morality . . . Frankness, sincerity, confidence, natural integrity, all the honourable affections were accused and denounced as silly, feeling is ridiculous, every scruple is a weakness, justice a superstition. Our interest or our pleasure alone should govern our actions. In short, it was the doctrine of disillusion and irresponsibility.

It is enlightening and not altogether unexpected to learn that M. de Voyer had many good and human qualities which he carefully kept out of sight. He was beneficent and just to the people of his estates and he secretly requested the blue riband[1] for himself from the King, although he was accustomed to deride the Court and the favours it granted. When the King

[1] The Order of the Saint Esprit, the highest order of the Monarchy. It was created by Henry III.

reproached him with corruption and refused the riband he died of the shock shortly afterwards. At least that was the reason given by his wife, who had the prettiest hands and feet and the longest nose[1] in Paris, and who ought to know.

After two years of events which are as monotonous to record as they must have become to live through, the young duke married Marie Adelaide, the only daughter of the Duke of Penthièvre, Grand Admiral of France and royal bastard of Louis XIV.

Besides being the richest heiress in the kingdom, probably in the world, she was a model of perfection. She was sixteen years old. Her figure was slight and the whiteness of her skin had that transparent quality that reveals the faint blue lace work of the veins beneath it. Her eyes were the colour of forget-me-nots and her gold hair formed an aureole of beauty about her gentle face. Her fresh lips had a smile of ingenuous sweetness and her hands were small and finely formed. Such is the ecstatic portrait of her drawn by the Comte Ducos.

She had been brought up in the strictest social and religious traditions which existed side by side with the profligacy and wit of the time and in such startling contrast to it that a sudden change from one world to the other often produced extravagant and unfortunate results. Philippe, already notorious for his scepticism, his gaiety and his charm, was as far removed both by nature and inclination from that respectable world as it was possible to be. Strangely

---

[1] Talleyrand. Harmand mentions the lady's nose.

35

enough, his father objected at first to the choice which the Abbé de Breteuil, the Chancellor of the House of Orléans, had fixed upon because the lady's father had been illegitimate, albeit royally so.

Moreover the greater part of the fortune seemed destined to go to the son, the Prince de Lamballe, a young man of twenty, far gone in debauchery. The negotiations languished. However, a few months later the Prince de Lamballe died of syphilis, and the immense size of the fortune which now descended upon Marie Adelaide determined the Duke of Orléans to reopen the question of his son's marriage. There was a lot of unpleasant back-stair diplomacy before it was decided. The enemies of Philippe Égalité, entirely ignoring dates, went so far as to say that he himself had purposely led his brother-in-law into the debauchery that resulted in his death—a charge which is mere invention. But it must be recorded for the very particular reason that the Queen was ready to believe it when the gossip was revived some years later by courtiers who had learned that any scandalous rumour about Philippe found a welcome listener in Marie Antoinette. It became, in fact, one of the earliest sources of that mutual hate which raged like an individual combat upon a vast battlefield and which only helped to lead both duellists to the scaffold. As for the truth of the accusation, the Duc de Penthièvre declared that Philippe would never have his son in his company, and the omnipresent Marais is so explicit as to give the name of the procureuse who was the means of producing the fatal illness.

36

Added to these witnesses is the fact that Philippe himself, twenty years of age, had no personal choice in his marriage, and at the time of the death of the Prince de Lamballe the whole thing was a matter of the vaguest conjecture in the mind of M. Breteuil.

The date of the wedding was finally fixed for April 5th, 1769, and at mid-day Philippe dressed in gold, and his bride dressed in white and silver, went to the altar with much splendour surrounding them. By some mistake Philippe was on the left side of Mlle de Penthièvre when they reached the altar. Some one leaned forward and told him, whereupon he jumped over the train of his bride's wedding dress on to the right side, an act which considerably shocked a number of ancient and respectable ladies who were present. As always the royal wedding was followed in detail by the public as well as by the Court. Pamphlets and broadsides took the place of newspapers. Some of them were rude and pointed out the "stupid array of lace embroideries, jewels and flowers worn by the bride." But most of them were rapturous with in-anities. You were told almost from minute to minute what the newly married couple were doing. Thus: The evening of the wedding the royal family meet the young Duc de Chartres and his new Duchess. After an hour or so at the royal gaming tables they sit down to supper, after which the King sends them each to prepare themselves for the night. The doors of the bedroom are opened with ceremony. The young couple kneel at the foot of the bed, which is then

37

blessed. The King stays to see them in bed, draws the bed-curtains himself, and "leaves the room with a patriarchal gesture."

The month is April; the year is 1769. Madame du Barry has just been installed in the apartment of the royal mistress. It is twenty years before the Revolution.

CHAPTER IV

THE PALAIS ROYAL

THE young Duc et Duchesse de Chartres established their home in the Palais Royal which, even more than Versailles, became a name to conjure with in the venturesome and uneasy years before the Revolution. 'If historians make it a point to seek the men whom they can award the honour or address the reproach of having made, directed or modified the French Revolution they will give themselves unnecessary trouble. It had no authors, leaders or guides. It was sown by the writers who, in an enlightened and daring century wishing to attack prejudices, subverted the religious and social principles, and by unskilful ministers who increased the deficit of the treasury and the discontent of the people.' A struggle, in fact, between the ideas of the intellectuals and those who held traditional power. Such is Talleyrand's verdict, and M. Gaxotte and other brilliant modern writers have done little more than to develop it. One after another the new men, the prophets of an unheard of heaven, appear in the salons of the Palais Royal. It was a natural centre to all that was in opposition, and the opposition could be to almost anything—religion, government or rank; the mere fact that they were in opposition gave them a sort of social standing which the liberal element among the aristocracy eagerly admitted. There has always been

PRINCE OF THE BLOOD

something superior about mixing titles with radicalism. The change and the growing pains of the century were not so much in debauchery as in debunking. Montesquieu, Buffon, Rousseau, Voltaire, Diderot, Condillac, d'Alembert, widely different though they were in personality and style, had in common that eagerness to attack tradition, that reputation of being philosophers which united them in the minds of the people both in the salons and in the street into an open conspiracy against all established authority. Not only in Paris, but all over France the new ideas of tolerence, liberty, and republicism spread and formed themselves into an ideal world that met in intellectual centres, reading clubs and literary societies. By belonging to the world of the new ideas people with drab lives became more than themselves, they walked in a golden light of hope, they were living for something beyond their own bread-winning, beyond their own niche in the social hierarchy. They belonged to a new order and they did not bother to inquire whether that new order might lead to the most colossal disorder, disaster and dissolution imaginable. It was enough to belong. Faith does far more than move mountains, it can upset empires and create worlds that reason declares to be manifestly impossible. In the presence of this dream world the commonplace world of everyday seemed to vanish and the romantic imagination painted everything with the hues of a new era. If it was Voltaire who delighted Paris by his impertinence and made aristocrats laugh at themselves with well-bred and sophisticated quips, it was Rousseau who produced the extraordinary wave of "feeling" that made an insincere sentimentality the order of the day. As Taine remarked, people who had been accustomed to get up in the early afternoon suddenly felt that they had been shown the splendour of a new dawn. There was a virtual organisation of brains to spread a sceptical materialism. Its opponents accused it of sowing moral corruption. But the gay world laughed—as Ségur wrote long afterwards!

"As for us young French nobles, without regret for the past, without misgivings for the future, we trod gaily on a carpet of flowers which hid the abyss from us. Laughing critics of the old fashions, of the feudal pride of our fathers and of their solemn rules of etiquette, all that was antique seemed to us tiresome and ridiculous. The gravity of the old doctrines oppressed us. Liberty, whatever language it might use, pleased us by reason of its boldness, equally by reason of its convenience. There is a pleasure in descending so long as one is certain of being able to rise again whenever one wants to do so; and so, blind to what was to befall, we enjoyed at one and the same time the advantages of a patrician status and the amenities of a plebian philosophy. Thus it was, that though it was our privileges and the relics of our former power that were being undermined beneath our feet, we took pleasure in this mimic warfare. We did not see its effect, we saw nothing by the spectacle; the form of the building remaining intact, we did not see that it was being undermined from within. We laughed at the grave alarms of the old court and the clergy who inveighed against this spirit of innovation. We applauded the republican scenes in our theatres, the philosophic discourses of our academies, the arduous writings of our men of letters. Combat with the pen and with words did not appear to us capable of damaging our existing superiority which several centuries of possession had made us regard as impregnable.

"We were bewildered by the prismatic hues of fresh ideas and doctrines, radiant with hopes, ardently aglow for every sort of reputation, enthusiastic for all talents and beguiled by every seductive dream of a philosophy that was about to secure the happiness of the human species . . . Free circulation was left to every reformative writing, to every prospect of innovation, to the most liberal ideas and to the boldest of systems. Everybody thought himself on the road to perfection without being under any embarrassment or feeling any kind of obstacle . . . Never was a more terrible awakening preceded by a sweeter slumber or by more seductive dreams."

When he was twenty-four years of age Philippe had an opportunity of adding to the reputation of the House of Orléans as the hereditary leader of the opposition to the Throne and the Government. His father had been sufficiently aroused from his natural indolence to take his place as head of the council of princes and magistrates of the high court, or Parlement of Paris, when the Chancellor Maupeou had brought about his *coup d'état* by attempting to abolish the parlements and thus securing absolute power for

Louis XV. Although Voltaire had a good word for Maupeou's move it was generally considered as a triumph for tyranny. Public feeling throughout the country rallied to the side of the parlements. It was, as a matter of fact, a struggle between two tyrannies. The prerogatives of the princes and the magistrates were based upon hereditary privilege, and favoured the people even less than the Government of the Crown. But as the magistrates were the only apparent opposition to a system of government which was becoming intolerable, it was natural for people to imagine that it possessed more virtue than it really did. Philippe joined in the fray with enthusiasm. His signature was upon all the letters of protest, which enraged Louis XV. He made himself conspicuous by defying petty restrictions. He earned himself a cheap popularity with the crowd by taking offence because a dogmatic sentry, interpreting his orders with great exactness, obliged his carriage to back away from the doors of the *Comédie Italienne*. His loss of temper was interpreted as noble defiance. He made himself further conspicuous by publicly ignoring his cousin, the Comte de la Marche, the only Prince who had refused to sign the protesting documents. Together with his father he refused to take his place in the new council which Maupeou attempted to establish in place of the former magistrates. For this both he and his father suffered exile for a time at the country estate of Villers-Cotterets near Paris. Although there was a reconciliation and the Orléans princes were received at Court towards the end of 1772, they did not alter their attitude to the

43

struggle and consistently ignored Maupeou's new council. When Louis XV. died, on May 10th of the following year, one of the first acts of the Duke of Orléans was to present to the young king, Louis XVI., "the prayers of the nation in the re-establishment of the former administration of justice to which the illustrious Court of Peers was inherent."

Louis XVI. hesitated to reply directly to this plea, although his adviser, Maurepas, was conservative by nature and only too ready to oppose Maupeou's reform and restore the former magistrates. The affair was further complicated as the princes of the blood refused to have any of their own legal claims or disputes settled before the Maupeou council. Moreover the Duke of Orléans and the Duc de Chartres refused to appear at the funeral of Louis XV., because they would be obliged to recognise publicly the existence of the Maupeou council which would be present officially. Louis XVI. replied by forbidding Philippe and his father from appearing at Court. The result was merely that "the popularity of the Orléans princes increased at the expense of the Court," the young Duc et Duchesse de Chartres were applauded in public while the young King and Queen were coldly received on their first drive across Paris on July 25th. Count Mercy, the Austrian Ambassador and councillor of Marie Antoinette, has a shrewd commentary upon the state of affairs. "The public," he wrote to his royal mistress Marie Thérèse on July 31st, "does not take any great interest in these two princes of the blood, but it is believed that their disgrace is the result of the zeal which they have shown for the former Parliament to which the people is more attached than ever."

But there was, in fact, no disgrace. The young people of Versailles and Palais Royal were not yet embittered, and Louis XVI. was perplexed and annoyed that he had had to punish his cousins and alienate the feelings of the Parisians. Moreover, the young pleasure-loving Queen disliked anything that disturbed the round of Court gaieties, and Philippe was one of the most sought after leaders of that world of pleasure. Maurepas soon understood the part he must play if he were to stay in his master's favour. The author of the new councils must be discredited. Accordingly Maupeou was manœuvred into a position whence he could conveniently be got rid of. It was rumoured that he was responsible for the libels on the young Queen which even at this early time were appearing in large numbers. Accordingly there was a reshuffling of ministers in which, to use a modern term, Maupeou was "liquidated." Louis XVI. announced that he intended to re-establish the parlements in the state in which they were before 1771, thus setting up the means by which the opposition would launch its first attack by his royal authority. By one of the strange ironies of history, the King was preparing the way to the revolution by his moderation and his liberal views rather than by any act of repression or tyranny.

Philippe's part in the affair is a minor one but it served to show the trend of his temper. His love of independence and popularity were confused between the essential and the trivial.

When he could not satisfy his craving for novelty he became intractable, and though in this first skirmish with the Court there were no very grievous wounds inflicted upon any one except Maupeou, it is nevertheless significant that Philippe had felt the check reins applied to himself. He had had his first taste of opposition in the world of pleasure that was slowly awakening to find itself a world of politics.

The Palais Royal was becoming the centre of that world. All that was brilliant, novel, witty and unconventional was certain of a welcome, and those who could produce the mythical rabbits from the hat of prodigality were hailed as benefactors of mankind.

Marie Adelaide, the young Duchesse de Chartres, as the mistress and rightful centre of this world, was woefully unsuited to her position, and as her husband was as slippery and difficult to control as mercury her task was impossible. She lacked the gay assurance of other ladies of her time. She needed the help of a stronger character to guide her, she had the sweetness of dependence, she wept easily, she was simple and affectionate—a girl who never quite grew up, and when she was faced with conflicting characters she retreated into a passive piety or resigned herself to suffering. The sophisticated world enjoyed her naïveté. Shortly after her marriage, as she was standing one evening at her window looking onto the gardens of the Palais Royal, one of her gentlemen-in-waiting seeing some courtesans pass by, remarked: " *Voilà des filles.*" " *Comment pouvez-vous savoir qu' elles ne sont pas mariées?*" asked the Duchesse, in her most candid ignorance. She was almost always "the estimable Duchesse de Chartres," sometimes merely "the poor Duchesse de Chartres," rather mute, heroic and inadequate both to herself and others. It needed a different type of woman to control, or rather to make the slightest impression on, the petulant and extravagant nature of Philippe. The most futile whims absorbed him—practical jokes, gambling and betting on any absurdity. For example, in 1777, while Lafayette and other Frenchmen were fighting in the American War, while the battle of the century, the battle for colonies and empire, was raging all over the western world, Philippe bet the Comte de Genlis that he could prick 500,000 holes in a piece of paper before that gentleman could go from the Palais Royal to Fountainebleau and back. He even went into training with a needle and paper—and he lost the bet.

CHAPTER V

ENTER THE HEROINE

SOME time during the spring of 1772 (there is some confusion about the exact date, nor does it matter very much) an event took place at the Palais Royal which on the face of it did not appear to be anything unusual but which was destined to alter profoundly the life of Philippe, and indeed to give a different tone to the society of the Palais Royal. The Duke of Orléans had appointed a witty, attractive young woman, la Comtesse de Genlis, to the household of his son, which he had every right to do. She was to be one of the ladies attending on the Duchesse de Chartres. *Cherchez la femme* is the proverbial French way to an explanation of almost anything, and although in Philippe's case it would be nearer the truth to say *Cherchez les femmes*, a special emphasis must fall on Mme de Genlis. " When one is a combination of ambition and moderation, observed Talleyrand, of communicativeness and reserve, of rigidity and complacency, one is certainly a person whose life and intimacy must offer extraordinary contrasts. It was by opposite means which she never separated that Madame de Genlis succeeded in all that her ambition desired. Being young, pretty, without relations, it was by risking morning calls to men that she found a husband: later she effected the height of prudery in a regular career of gallantries: with the same pen she wrote *Knights of the Swan* and *Lessons in Morals for Children*: on the same desk she composed a church book for Mlle de Chartres and a speech to the Jacobins for the Duke of Orléans." All her life presents the same contrasts. In her memoirs, composed when she was an old and famous lady who had written a remarkable number of books on manners and education, survived a revolution, educated a king, been pensioned by Napoleon and made an enormous number of enemies, she is so discreet and so consciously vague about the details of her own life that it is impossible to verify Talleyrand's remarks. However, it is quite certain that Félicité du Crest was married quite correctly to the Comte de Genlis, later Marquis de Sillery, and that she bore him two children. According to gossip her husband was cursed with the passion for gambling which outweighed even that for women. Félicité was of inferior birth and in considerable poverty at the time of her marriage and, her husband being a nobleman, she was able for the first time to play a part in the great and gay world of society. Although there were some rumblings among the dowagers, and her husband's family would not receive her for several months, she rapidly succeeded in making a place for herself by her charm and her eccentricities.

She followed all the activities of the time with eagerness and ability, she was an accomplished harpist, she wore trousers on occasions and took baths in milk strewn with rose petals which, according to her own opinion, "is one of the most agreeable things to do in the world."

Her expression was intelligent, she had good humour but her wit even as a young woman was very caustic. She felt the lack of sympathy about her but she was determined to overcome it.

Even after a presentation at Court she did not feel securely launched in society, and it was not until she was appointed to the household of the Duchesse de Chartres that she began to win her battles. She was twenty-two years old. "Her figure," wrote the Duchesse d'Abrantès, "was slender and prettily rounded, her face had a piquant expression which, added to the spirit of observation which dominated everything in this pretty head, made her singularly attractive." She took care to get her husband appointed to the Palais Royal as a Captain of the Guards at the same time as she took her position as lady-in-waiting. It was an act of policy rather than affection.

When exactly Philippe fell in love with her is uncertain. Probably it was at a ball at the opera some time before she entered the household of the Palais Royal. Mme de Genlis had composed some music for a ballet in which she herself was to dance in the costume of a peasant girl. As the opening notes sounded the howling of a cat in the gallery began softly and rose to enormous proportions, ruining the piece. Attendants who captured the "cat" found it to be a child, paid by Philippe to spoil the fun because he had not been asked to help in the management of the party.

Observation and love of power soon brought their rewards to the young lady-in-waiting. The group of

ladies around the Duchesse de Chartres was chiefly
composed of conservative and respectable great dames
whose pronouncements were always in good taste and
often dull. Philippe delighted in shocking them with
paradoxes that scoffed at tradition and ridiculed
sentiment. He would stride up and down the salon, tall,
vigorous, alert, somewhat haughty, and meeting with
nothing but raised eyebrows or condescending and
deprecatory smiles he would become ribald. One of the
young ladies, Mlle de Blot, very beautiful, languising
and ethereal, hoped to draw Philippe into the heaven
of her ideal love. The appearance of Mme de Genlis
produced a pronounced change. Besides her obvious
social charm she had a mind that was eager for knowledge. Little by little she made herself indispensable
to the Duchesse de Chartres. She was serious and gay by
turns. When she talked about literature she was
instructive as well as witty; she was eloquent upon
education and earnest upon religion. Years later
Horace Walpole called her a hen Rousseau, but now
she was in the pullet stage. Her harp-playing reached
the excellence of a professional musician. The Duchesse
was charmed. Her pious nature longing to depend on
some one, grew more and more attached to the
estimable countess. Mlle de Blot faded into a languishing heaven of her own, unwept for.

Under the influence of the gay and charming new-
comer the Palais Royal became a rival centre to the
court at Versailles where the young Dauphine Marie
Antoinette was casting the spell of her incredible
beauty on all who came to do homage. At the Palais

Royal Mme de Genlis was supreme. She held receptions, she received the celebrated Buffon, she watched over the Duchesse. Indeed the dear Duchesse soon came to depend upon her new friend for everything. "Every day, if anything out of the ordinary occurred to her, she told me of it," wrote Mme de Genlis, "and sent for me to consult me or to confide in me what interested her. It very often happened that she sent me Mlle Lefèvre, one of the ladies of her chamber, at two or three in the morning when I had not been able to see her during the day."

There were Tuesday conversations when the wit and learning of an age blossomed under her smile, her shrewd answers and her intelligence. Women point to the power of the vote as the crowning achievement that has made them the equals of men as though there were something strange and noble in such a ludicrous position. In the salons of Paris at the end of the old order of things the women were the masters as well as the mistresses, of men, and never did they wield their despotism with more power, more charm or more grace.

"It is very difficult nowadays," wrote Mme Vigée Lebrun, forty years later, "to give any idea of the urbanity and graceful ease of the manners which were the great charm of Parisian society. This politeness of which I speak has totally disappeared. Women reigned then, the Revolution dethroned them."

There are glimpses of many faces in the brightly-lighted salons of the Palais Royal, many among them destined to look across the gulf of blood that seemed then so impossibly remote. Bailly the astrologer expounded his theory of the stars, Hérault de Séchelles his theory of women—the one very new, the other immemorial. Bailly the mild dreamer and future mayor of the Revolution, destined to be dragged through the mud of the Paris streets and guillotined one freezing, wet afternoon on a dungheap. "Bailly, you tremble," taunted one of the murderous rabble as the guillotine was being set up. "My friend," replied the old man, "if I tremble, it is with cold." Hérault de Séchelles, maker of mystical constitutions, future president of a doomed Convention, was destined also to be dragged through the crowded streets but in a tumbril, one April afternoon when all the chestnut trees were in blossom and the soft spring air would make him think of love, as it always did, in spite of this tiresome business of getting one's head cutoff .It was he who embraced Danton as they mounted the steps of the streaming guillotine one after another, who waved his hand gaily, it was said, to some one high up at one of the windows before it was tied behind him. Now he pays compliments to Mme de Genlis while she ponders to herself an important question. She has been complimented for her harp-playing by no less a person than Marie Antoinette herself—moreover the royal compliment had included an invitation to the clever countess to play at Versailles. She decided to refuse. "I had ties enough," she wrote, "not to wish for others. This would have taken up an enormous amount of my time and so would have upset my studies. So I allowed no further steps to be taken in the affair." It sounds ingenuous but it is merely ingenious. At Versailles she would have been a planet revolving in the sunlight of the future queen. At the Palais Royal she was the sunlight itself and already even the unstable course of Philippe was moving with some regularity around her. People remarked that there was a dangerous warmth. Yet everything was so discreet and so well-bred. Mme de Genlis was so evidently attached to the Duchesse de Chartres. Even biographers were uncertain for the next hundred years. No one could say for certain what was true, that Philippe and Félicité, Comtesse de Genlis were passionately in love.

CHAPTER VI

TRIANGLES AND TRAVEL

PHILIPPE did not know how to resist the woman who knew how to lead him. All his life he lived in the shadow of something—his heritage, his name, his vanity, his horses, Mme de Genlis, anglomania, the guillotine. The woman who knew how to lead him had now appeared, and she not only led him, she ruled him in thought and in action, in detail and in general policy, so that people wondered that this puppet of inconstancy could become so stable or so attached. But she did it circumspectly.

She was so much his superior in intelligence and in self-control that it was natural, not difficult, for her to do so. Love of power and control of others were necessary to her. But under the gushing insincerity which was the fashion à la Jean-Jacques Rousseau, she loved him.

Knowledge of this love affair came about in a curious way. The Duchesse de Chartres was in poor health, she was childless and she was suffering from bad teeth. To remedy the childlessness she went to Forges to take the waters which had proved so beneficient to Anne of Austria. Naturally her dear friend Mme de Genlis went with her, as did her languishing rival Mme de Blot. Somewhat less naturally Philippe accompanied the party. All this is

mentioned quite casually in the memoirs and no reader
of Mme de Genlis's account could possibly deduce
anything but the monotony of the journey and the
virtue of the waters. When they had been at Forges
for a fortnight Philippe had to return to the Palais
Royal to be present at the confinement of his sister,
the Duchesse of Bourbon. During the following days
the secret police of Louis XV. whose duty it was to
inform the King of the activities of his subjects,
especially those of the rival branch of the royal house,
intercepted and copied a series of love-letters between
Philippe and the young countess, which removed any
doubt about their being lovers and must have caused
some royal amusement. More than a century later
they were discovered by a French scholar[1] in the
dusty files of diplomatic papers in the Foreign Office
archives, among a wilderness of polite notes and
formal suggestions. Perhaps as love-letters they are
not very extraordinary or very different from other
love-letters—but like other love-letters they are
passionate with life and they bring out sudden,
humorous and otherwise hidden traits of character
meant only for the eyes of one person, and understood
by the whole world. A man's character is not entirely
lost if he can love, no matter what ignominy the
world hangs on him.

   "Oh, *mon enfant, mon cœur*," wrote Mme de Genlis,
"to love with such excess, to give oneself up to
love so entirely one should be certain of never

---

[1] The correspondence was published by Gaston Maugras in a slim volume
called *L'Idylle d'un Gouverneur*. M. Mangras is triumphantly shocked and
righteously severe in his judgment.

being away from each other for more than two days.

"I have given myself, abandoned myself to you in a transport of delight.

"Never was friend or child loved like you. Love me always as you do now. Be always so lovely to me, so charming, so tender, and it is impossible that I should ever complain no matter what happens to me."

The letters also contain references to the Duchesse's teeth and complained of the smell of ether which she was using to stop the pain.

Philippe's answers were ardent and condoling. "How tender, lovable, and charming you are, my child," he wrote. "Your letter enchants me. It causes me a singular pleasure to see that we both wrote the same things to each other at practically the same moment." About the Duchesse's teeth he was less gallant and wrote that he hoped the dentist, le Chevalier de Durfort, would pull them all out, "And I would not be sorry," he added, "if the tongue went with them."

In her letter to Philippe, written on the same day, Mme de Genlis had said, "I love behaviour that is honest and, above all, noble."

And he, the hardened cynic, the mould of fashion, the disillusioned, declares that he wants nothing more than to shut himself up in his room to think about his love. M. de Voyer's doctrine breaks down at the first assault of feeling. Apparently he was very pleased with his own letters, because Mme de Genlis assures him that when they are published she will leave out the indiscretions and edit them with great care.

"I don't understand, my child," she complained, "why you only have six letters from me and I have eight from you. Certainly I have written more."

Sometimes she mixed another tone in her love letters. She liked nothing better than the chance to instruct some one sweetly but firmly, particularly in morals. It was not mere unpleasantness which made one of her enemies refer to her as the most learned of all the learned ladies, past, present and probably to come.

She had no idea of getting rid of the Duchesse de Chartres in order to replace her. Instead she wrote her lover an enthusiastic letter commending his wife's character and reproving him for neglecting her. "I do not approve at all of your conduct," she wrote, "and I expect to see you repair this negligence which afflicts me. You are mine, you are mine and I am always sure beforehand that you will do everything that I desire." In another letter, she added a little moral lesson on the purity, honesty and sensibility of his wife's nature and begged him to reflect upon it. Indeed it was one of the strangest triangles in the world.

A few days before she left Forges she wrote: "My mourning is coming to an end," and added, "I seem to have read that somewhere, but as you never read anything, you couldn't tell me where."

"I received your last letter, my dear child, and here is mine," she wrote on August 12th. "We are leaving for Dieppe to-morrow at ten o'clock in the evening, and for Paris at nine o'clock in the morning. We will arrive about ten o'clock in the evening. I will go and shut myself in my room at once.

"They send me news from Paris that M. de Genlis should arrive on the 17th. If that is so he will know by Saint-Jean the day I am arriving and he will not fail to be at the Palais Royal. I will have the pretext of fatigue to get rid of him by eleven-thirty. Come softly, and if the door is shut, *mon enfant* will wait and imagine to himself that there will be behind that door a heart as agitated and impatient as his own.

"Adieu, *cher enfant*—Oh! Sunday as you say— what shall we become."

This was the last letter of the correspondence.

The Duchesse de Chartres gave birth to a son on October 6th, 1773. Her dear friend was always with her. The following year another son was born, followed by twin girls in 1777, and a third son in 1779. The waters of Forges and the little moral lessons had been efficacious.

The correspondence was renewed during Philippe's absence, but the letters took on a slightly more formal tone. "Madame and Monseigneur" replaced "mon enfant, mon cœur." Philippe often exaggerated his indifference to the point of crudity. "Mme de Genlis of the Palais Royal," wrote a gossip of the salons, in May, 1773, "has been very ill with measles; her son died of it. These two events have occasioned neither sorrow nor anxiety nor pain to M. le Duc de Chartres, which astonishes every one because he has been sub- jugated and led by her for a long time. This proves that he is weak and hasn't any heart. I knew it a long time ago."

Philippe was in Bruxelles in July, and certainly his letters mention nothing about Mme de Genlis's misfortune. Instead they are full of an egotistical restlessness. "I confess," he wrote, "that my taste for travel grows every day. I enjoy more and more leaving one place and arriving at another. Yet I know I will grow sick of it here in a fortnight." He often travelled under the name of the Comte de Joinville in order to escape the fêtes and ceremonies, the reviews of troops, the civic welcomes and all the formalities due to a prince of the blood. This restlessness and curiosity became the source of a second education. He was popular in the country—he was the gay young prince of the House of Orléans, who rode well, laughed easily, and whose hair was growing a little thin on his forehead. It was even said that numbers of young men plucked their foreheads in order to be in the fashion. During the spring and summer months his coach rushed through the warm nights along the great straight roads of France from one end of the kingdom to the other; to Brest, to Toulon, to Holland, to Brussels, or on shorter journeys to Villers-Cotterets, to Fontainbleau, to Compiègne — always at full gallop, with two outriders dashing ahead, and inside, a single valet and perhaps a friend such as Biron or Fitzjames, always returning in a few weeks, forgetting sometimes why they had set out. His endurance was exceptional, but he scarcely knew what he wanted to endure beyond the gratification of the moment. At

Spa he stayed three August days and was charmed by the prodigious assembly of different nationalities. "After thirty-one hours travel," he wrote, "I thought I should be fatigued . . . I dined like an ogre and then went to the casino where I watched some English girls dance for three hours or so." He made friends with every one, he wrote the Duchesse that he had tried all the waters, that there were many amiable people but very few pretty women. He left again two days later.

Madame de Genlis neither languished nor betrayed any irritation at Philippe's waywardness. From 1769-1777 she became the fashion in Paris. She devoted herself to the theatre and to education. The *élite* of the social and intellectual world flocked to her readings, receptions and theatricals to enjoy themselves and praise their hostess. She composed moral plays in which her young daughters and other children acted. A hall seating five hundred people was too small to hold the throng that came to applaud. Grimm praised her. Rousseau thought her the long lost Julie of his dreams and then, as usual, turned on her and declared she had persecuted him. Voltaire, upon the occasion of a visit from her at Ferney, declared he would give up his slippers and dressing-gown and appear again in the great world. She became the crusader against vice and against evil passions. She also began to acquire that touch of pendantry which grew as she grew older and more celebrated. And she had strengthened her already unassailable position by becoming the governess of the children of the Duc et Duchesse de Chartres.

In fact she was proceeding with a calculating and profound assurance. She might not be able to be Philippe's only lover. That was expecting the impossible, and besides, there were more important things than that. It was more important, for example, to remain the most influential, the most feared and the most necessary person in the Orléans family. The jealousy she had aroused in the Palais Royal already rivalled the enmity she called forth from the Court. But as governess of the royal children she could retire into a safe world which she could rule with absolute discretion.

CHAPTER VII

AT SEA

" Am I to be condemned to eternal idleness?" wrote Philippe in 1772. " Even if war should come what could I hope to do? I am twenty-five years old and I have not seen service yet. The navy is my only resource —it is the only part I could take to acquire public esteem and consideration, without which our birthright only puts us lower than others."

There is more than mere self-indulgence and vanity in this letter; there is, in fact, the first evidence of an ambition which in itself was estimable and which made Philippe the only Royal Prince to embrace any of the new ideas but which was backed up by so much ill judgment that it recoiled upon itself with grotesque results.

Philippe's naval career began in 1772 when he took part as a volunteer in the summer manœuvres of a squadron under the command of d'Orvilliers. His appearance at Brest was greeted with enthusiasm. He began as a simple *garde de la marine* and was promoted *Ensign de vaisseau* at the end of the cruise. In 1775 he sailed on board the *Tourterelle* and the *Terpsichore*, and it is interesting to learn that he preferred to use his pseudonym of Joinville rather than his royal title.

He showed at once a decided taste for the Navy and

all the exercises and manœuvres which go with it. Moreover, the Minister of Marine was informed that there was "no one great or small who has not been honoured by marks of his goodness." At the end of this second cruise which extended to la Coroque, he was made *Capitaine de vaisseau*.

On his return to Paris the King wrote to him to tell him that his example was most useful to his service. "I learned with pleasure," added Louis, "that you were not made ill by the sea and that you were in excellent health—a great asset in following the career you have begun."

The following year, on April 1st, 1776, he was promoted to the rank of *chef d'escadre des armiés navales* and sailed in the *Solitaire* from Brest to Lisbone thence to Cape St. Vincent, where the ship received orders to join another squadron from Toulon. An outbreak of scurvy developed on board the *Solitaire* and the admiral in command, Le Comte Duchaffault, reported the fact to the Minister, and added that if it continued he "would try to find a way of putting the person of monseigneur le duc de Chartres in safety." But Philippe refused to abondon his command. The *Solitaire* was obliged to remain for some time at Lagos, and a letter which Philippe sent to his admiral throws an altogether new light on his character. "Sir," he wrote, "I have not put the sick men ashore as you advised me and as I had intended to do, because the ship's surgeon informed me that if he landed the drugs and mattresses necessary he would not have enough left in case of further sickness at sea. Besides, he considered it a useless precaution as the men have much improved, except eight, and he does not give up hope about these. Furthermore it has been suggested to me that if the health officer inland, upon examining them, declares that there is an epidemic, it will cut all communication between the squadron and the land. These reasons decided me to leave the men on board although it annoys me somewhat because I shall have to stay here at least eight days, and I am most anxious to find myself under your orders, sir, and to instruct myself by your example. I hope that you do not in any way doubt this, nor the feeling of esteem which I have for you. If you still desire to complete our cruise I will leave port in eight or ten days and will wait for you outside Lagos, cruising as far as Cape St. Mans unless you order otherwise. Signed, L.P. Joseph d'Orléans.

Towards the end of May the *Solitaire* was able to sail, and on the 28th Philippe commanded the man-œuvres of the entire squadron with considerable ability, although there was some trouble on June 1st, when the *Solitaire* collided with the *Terpsichore*, an accident which Philippe promptly admitted was his own fault. But it was the general opinion that M. le Duc de Chartres had shown great firmness of character during the cruise which the Admiral Duchaffault had no hesitation in pronouncing one of the hardest he had ever made.

Why should Philippe have chosen to serve in the Navy? Until now no prince of the blood had ever done so. The sea has never seemed the natural kingdom of the French. All the dash and fire, the precision and amazing flair which have gone to make the French armies and French staff work the finest in history seem to become subdued on the sea. At Yorktown, de Grasse was successful it is true, but he was restless and nervous, and shortly after lost his entire fleet to Rodney. And Villeneuve only fought at Trafalgar when he was stung into action by Napoleon's fierce gibes. So natural was it to Frenchmen to think in terms of the army rather than of the navy that before 1791 the rank corresponding to rear-admiral was known as lieutenant-general of the naval armies.

But the reason for Philippe's choice was not unnatural. His father-in-law, the Duc de Bourbon Penthièvre, held the highest naval rank in the kingdom —Grand Admiral of France. He had never been on a ship, though he had had a toy flotilla built at Brest and brought to his estate at Rambouillet, where it was launched in the canals and where he could study interesting naval tactics. The position of Admiral of France was one of great prestige and considerable profit. The revenue in 1788, for example, reached the large sum of four hundred thousand livres.[1]

Philippe would be the natural successor to this title especially if he took the unusual course of actually going to sea. He might well replace his father-in-law before that gentleman died. Rumours of this were used to stir up bad feeling between the Duc de Pen-

[1] A tenth of the prizes and prisoners of war, fines imposed in various edicts connected with the Admiralty and a third of all *épaves* were the sources of the income.

thièvre and Philippe. Thus far the King had appeared to be favourable to his career, but how long he or the Queen would be willing to contemplate the idea of such a powerful position being controlled by the House of Orléans was highly uncertain.

The American Revolution had roused French feeling to a dangerous state. Franklin had arrived in Paris and was pleading the American cause to willing listeners. News of the capture of General Burgoyne and the British army at Saratoga on the 16th October, 1777, had produced a sensation, and on the 6th February, Louis XVI. formally received the American Commissioners and signed a treaty of recognition and friendship. War with England was now certain. These events had enormously increased the importance of the navy and Philippe was more than ever determined to play a part in it. He was promoted to the rank of *Lieutenant-Général des Armées Navales* and left for Brest on May 16th, arrived on the 19th and went on board the *Saint Esprit*, the flagship of the third division. The Minister of Marine, Sartine, urged him to use his influence to heal the dissensions which existed between the regular naval officers, who were required to show proofs of aristocracy, and the auxiliary officers of the Merchant Marine, who were treated by them as intruders. It was the inevitable *esprit de corps* destroying a necessary co-operation for a larger aim, and it is significant to learn that Philippe was able to break down this snobbery by showing no preference for one caste or the other and inviting them to his table indiscriminately.

Across the Channel at Plymouth lay the English fleet under the command of their most able seaman, Admiral Keppel.

Both sides were eager for hostilities to begin. It only needed an excuse to set the two fleets in motion. On June 17th, a chance encounter between the French frigate *La Belle Poule* and the English frigate *Arethusa* was the signal for hostilities. On July 8th, twenty-seven ships of the French fleet hoisted sail and put out of Brest into the Channel to look for Keppel and his ships.

Philippe commanded the third division. The moment seemed to be approaching when his ambition for public esteem and consideration was about to be realised and his dreams of being Admiral of France near to reality.

Away on the English coast Keppel had given his sailing orders and thirty English warships slipped out of Plymouth, led by the *Victory*, of a hundred guns.

And yet within a month Philippe's career had ended in a ludicrous mess and so far from being made Grand Admiral of France he was appointed Colonel-General of Huzzars on land at his own request, and within a year he had the mortification to receive a letter from Marie Antoinette informing him that the King forbade him from taking any further active part in the war whatsoever.

Like everything else he did the beginning was good, he even attained a certain distinction, and then all was lost in a welter of gossip and calumny which his ineptness in defending himself only served to aggravate. It is not so difficult apparently to win golden opinions as to keep them from being replaced by counterfeits. Philippe after the battle of Ushant is a subject to make grave philosophers stroke their beards in wonder.

CHAPTER VIII

THE BATTLE OF USHANT

THE Kings of France and England having gravely insulted each other, and having informed their admirals that it was lawful, honourable and urgent to fall upon, seize and destroy each other's ships, the two fleets cruised in the Channel waiting for the chance to join in battle. The descriptions of the fight that took place on July 27th are so varied, the exaggerations by each side so picturesque, and the results so negligible, that it can almost be claimed that the chief result of this sea fight was to lose Philippe his naval career. One thing is certain—the weather was blowing a heavy gale on Thursday, July 23rd, when Keppel discovered the French fleet working to windward and sailed in pursuit. The gale blew exceedingly hard until the 26th, while some eighty warships thrashed their way down the Channel manœuvring for a favourable position. So high was the wind that the French ships, which were to windward, were lying over so far that they lost the use of their lower batteries. The great cloud of sail, the sense of speed as the ships plunged ahead, the approach of the battle made Philippe's blood tingle. There are reports of him talking eagerly with his Captain, La Motte Picquet and le Comte de Genlis on the quarter-deck, and as the wind was still strong and there seemed to be little chance of closing with the enemy, he signalled a message to Olliviers urging him to give orders that would bring on the action. According to custom, he was dressed in the brilliant white uniform of a lieutenant-general and wore the blue ribbon—the highest order of the kingdom. There was still a certain ceremony about going into battle which gas, machine-guns and long range artillery have since made ridiculous but which at least made "the glorious pursuit of war" more personal and picturesque than it has since become.

On August 3rd, the *Morning Post* in London, under the heading "News from Keppel," printed the following account:

"Monday (the 27th) the gale abating early in the morning the enemy steered a leeward course and drew up in the line of battle. (A magnificent sight and excellently performed, reported a British Naval Officer who witnessed the manœuvre). Immediately on perceiving this Mr. Keppel gave the signal for running to windward of them and came to a general action which was effected as far as *Gaellic heroism* would permit, for the French soon crowded all their sails and *gallantly* ran into Brest harbour, but not till they were pretty severely handled.

"His Royal Highness, the Duc de Chartres, had a grapple with the *Victory* but thought proper to retire on receiving her fourth broadside, with the rest of her squadron, leaving once more the British flag to ride in triumph before Brest."

This superior British scorn covered an almost complete falsification of the facts. Philippe's ship, the

Saint Esprit, scarcely took part in the actual fighting owing to the various manœuvres which left him and his squadron on the fringe of the battle. The ship which engaged the *Victory* was the *Bretagne* carrying the Admiral Olliviers who commanded the entire fleet. But the London papers seemed impressed by the presence of a prince of the blood and insisted on making him the commander-in-chief, as though there were more honour in defeating royalty than a mere French admiral.

Two days later, August 6th, the *Morning Chronicle*, finding it utterly impossible to believe in anything but victory, reported that the French had lost one thousand two hundred dead and two thousand wounded—a fantastic statement as the actual number officially given by Olliviers was one hundred and sixty-three dead and one hundred and seventeen wounded.

By this time the French accounts began to reach London. On August 7th, the *Morning Post* printed a translation from the *Gazette de France* which was exactly opposite to the English account. "The King's army," it read, "pursued that of England and constantly offered them battle in the best order, but the English admiral doubtless did not think it fit to accept it and availed himself of the darkness of the night to effect his retreat by carefully hiding his fires, while all the ships of the King's army carried them that their positions might be clearly perceived by the English army."

The mere suggestion that the French could be right caused the *Morning Chronicle* on the following day to snort with rage against the foreigners. "The great rejoicings of the French nation for the complete victory gained over the English and the defeat of our best admiral in the Navy, as given out by their ministry and as greedily swallowed by the misled and infatuated slaves of that arbitrary country, thoroughly evince their being made up of fallacies, superstitions, gasconades and cowardice."

Keppel's official report, dated, " *Victory*, at sea, July 30, 1778," was almost as vague. The position where the battle took place, the number of ships engaged, sunk or captured is left entirely to the imagination. He reported one hundred and thirty-three dead and three hundred and seventy-three wounded. He declared that he had allowed the French to reform towards the close of the day without firing on them, "thinking they meant handsomely to try their force with us the next morning, but they had been so beaten in the day that they took the advantage of the night to move off.

"The wind and weather being such that they could reach their own shores before there was any chance of the King's fleet getting up with them, the state that the ships were in, in their masts, yards and sails, left me no choice of what was proper and advisable to do"—which was to sail back to Plymouth.

No ship on either side was sunk or taken as a prize. Both admirals claimed that they had pursued the enemy and both asserted that the opposing fleet had stolen away in the night, and there was rejoicing in both countries—but not for long.

This drawn, glorious and rather futile sailing bout

may have saved a few East Indiamen, but "contrary-wise" from a military point of view it left matters where they were before. France was still free to communicate with America whose cause she was supporting.

On the 31st Keppel had anchored off Plymouth, and the evening before Philippe had obtained permission to carry his version of victory to Paris. It is from that moment that his real and unfortunate part in the naval battle of Ushant may be said to begin. There was considerably more fighting on paper afterwards than there ever had been from the decks of the warships —a phenomenon not unknown in our own time.

During the evening of August 1st Philippe made his report to the King at Versailles and the following day returned to the Palais Royal, where a vast crowd cheered him and refused to disperse until he had appeared on the balcony. Songs were sung about "a hero worthy of the blood of our kings." Keppel was burnt in effigy in the gardens of the Palace and two evenings later at the Opera there were scenes of great enthusiasm and cheers for the young and brave warrior. At the end of a triumphant evening he left for Brest. On August 17th the fleet again put to sea to protect French merchant shipping and capture English prizes, but after cruising in thick fog for some time returned to Brest on September 17th having accomplished nothing.

Philippe left at once for Paris, where he found a very different reception waiting for him. During his absence the true nature of the encounter had filtered through. The two brothers of the King, the Comte

74

d'Artois and Monsieur, jealous of Philippe's success, were not slow in sneering at him. The Minister of Marine Sartine was improvident enough to publish one of several reports of his Admiral Olliviers, in which the Duc de Chartres was mentioned as having put off the victory through a misreading of signals. The tongue of every gossip started wagging—They say there were only four wounded and one killed on the *Saint Esprit*—They say he sailed in the wrong direction —They say he was kept out of it purposely by Olliviers himself—They say he hid in the hold during the entire action . . . etc. etc.[1]

The texts of the admiral's reports are enough to disprove any charge of failure in line of duty or of personal cowardice. In a report on July 29th, Olliviers declared that he would have had a success glorious to the French flag if the enemy had accepted the second encounter during the afternoon—that same afternoon during which Keppel says he did not fire because he thought the French would look handsome on the following day. Two days later Olliviers shifted the blame for Keppel's unwillingness to fight to the slowness of the Duc de Chartres in responding to certain signals, and twelve days later he modified his statement as far as to say that whatever mistakes there

[1] It is a curious coincidence that the British blamed the indecisive action upon exactly the same cause—a slowness or a refusal to obey signals by Sir Hugh Palliser, third in command and one of the Lords of the Admiralty. There was a violent quarrel between him and Keppel which developed into a party fight, Keppel being a Whig and Palliser a Tory. There were stormy debates in Parliament. Keppel was court-martialled in 1779 and honourably acquitted. Palliser's house was attacked by a mob, which then proceeded to the Admiralty and hurled bricks through the windows. Palliser, who was inside with his mistress, beat an undignified retreat across the horse-guards parade, showing evident signs of terror.

might have been were due to the inevitable confusion of a general action. This was the so-called official version of the affair as given by Olliviers and Sartine. But in the royal inquiry held at Brest at the King's orders, Philippe's conduct was put above blame and his capacity praised by every one of the captains who took part in the battle. The King was entirely satisfied but the public scented scandal and, true or false, it determined to pursue it and its victim.

The Minister Sartine made this possible. He could save his own position and that of his favourite admiral by throwing the blame of an inconclusive action upon the Duc de Chartres. It did not matter that La Motte Picquet and the Vicomte Laval, both of whom were on board the *Saint Esprit*, were ready to declare that it was Philippe himself who had urged on Olliviers to action—it did not matter that there were various denials of the existence of the signals supposed to have been ignored, or that Philippe was credited with "a cool and tranquil courage and an astonishing presence of mind." One report, somewhat exaggerated it is true, spoke of seven large ships, one a three-decker, successfully attacking M. le Duc de Chartres, "who replied with great vigour although he had lost his lower batteries."

But Philippe had lost far more than his lower batteries—he had lost his head as well. He did not follow up the proposal of his friends at the Palais Royal to print the log of La Motte Picquet as well as the result of the Royal inquiry. This undoubtedly would have completely shattered the charges in the

"official" report of Sartine and Olliviers and re-
instated him in the public esteem. But in order to save
his own skin Sartine declared to the King that it was
impossible to discredit the admiral at this point in the
war, and the weak and well-meaning King ordered
that nothing further should be printed concerning the
Ushant affair. Instead of fighting the intrigue,
Philippe now made an incredibly stupid move with
the best intentions in the world. He wrote the King
a letter full of bitterness in which he said frankly that
he had had every intention of proving himself worthy
of inheriting the title of Grand Admiral, but that
instead of achieving his hope his position and his
reputation were compromised, the esteem of his
father-in-law was forfeited and the fate of his wife and
children imperilled. In order to restore himself, and as
a public evidence of the King's satisfaction, he asked to
be given the rank of Colonel-General of Huzzars. As a
recognition of service in the Navy it was ludicrous, and
the ironic humour of the request was not long in
appearing. Many people, in fact, considered that it had
been devised by Marie Antoinette in particular to
show the Court's contempt. It is true that the Queen
must have been well aware of the incongruity of the
request. In fact she urged Louis to grant it, and it only
adds to the irony to know that it originated not with
her but with Philippe himself. The King made the
following note at the foot of Philippe's letter. "The
King wishing to give an evidence of his satisfaction
and prove that he is equally content with his zeal and
the capacity which he has shown in his service upon all

occasions, particularly at the battle of Ushant of July 27th, creates for him the rank of Colonel-General of Huzzars and Light Troops, etc."

This apparent benevolence had poison in it.

The Minister of War, M. Montbarry, had no idea of getting himself or his department involved in the same sort of trouble as M. Sartine had been through. Nor had the King and Queen any idea of letting Philippe attract any more attention that might flatter the name of Orléans. Just a year after he had returned in triumph from the battle of Ushant he received the following letter written in the Queen's hand.

The King has been informed and is displeased, sir, with your intention of joining his army. The constant refusal which he has deemed it necessary to make to the most earnest entreaties; the consequences which your example would entail have made it only too clear to me that he will admit neither excuse nor indulgence. The affliction which I feel because of this had determined me to accept the commission of informing you of his intentions which are very positive. He has thought that by sparing you the severe form of an order that he would diminish the chagrin of his contradiction without delaying your submission. Time will prove that I have only consulted your interest and that upon this occasion as upon all others, I will also endeavour, sir, to prove my sincere affection for you.

MARIE ANTOINETTE

As Philippe read this letter he must have felt the

queenly defiance behind it and realised that, as Mirabeau remarked later, "*Le roi n'a qu'un homme, c'est sa femme.*"

Philippe has been supposed to be one of the most able, insidious and diabolical intriguers of the Revolution. He was, in fact, one of the most inept. Once again the Court had checked him and he was not likely to forget it, nor to reflect that it was largely his own blundering that had brought it about.

CHAPTER IX

NOT TO EXCUSE BUT TO EXPLAIN

THE importance of this naval exploit in Philippe's development can hardly be exaggerated. His sudden revulsion from the intrigue of the Ministry was partly a misplaced disdain for the opinion fostered by his enemies and partly inverted sensibility fed by the doctrine of disillusionment. Morally it left him more stranded than ever before. The world of action was suddenly closed to him and rather than brave the tension of a long drawn out trial of strength he preferred to fall back on mediocrity which always prefers an easy existence and satisfies its vanity in pleasure. Marie Antoinette's letter marks the open division between the Palais Royal and the Court. From then on the Palais Royal became the rallying point of the Revolution and Philippe was gradually thrust into a leadership for which he was totally unfitted, a political leadership of all those who wished to oppose the ruling house of the Bourbons (which in public opinion was becoming more and more dominated by the " Austrian wench ") of all those who favoured liberal ideas, a limited monarchy, liberty, equality and democracy, in fact any of the ideas that men contemplated when they looked across the Channel to England or still farther across the ocean to America. Powerful, widespread and dangerous to all established forms was this

MARIE ADELAIDE, DUCHESS OF CHARTRES

opposition. "The critical mind prevailed everywhere, everybody prided himself on being an opponent, it was the general disposition; it animated all the corporations, it prevailed in all the writings; all men vied with each other as to who should attack a ministry that no one dared to defend and which, after all, perhaps had no more dangerous enemy than its own incapacity."

The greatest confidence accompanied this spirit of criticism. Never, says Taine, was an aristocracy so deserving of power at the moment of losing it. The powerful class aroused from their indolence were again becoming public men and, restored to their functions, were returning to their duties. Never were the French so combined together to combat the evils to which nature makes us pay tribute and those which in a thousand ways creep into all social institutions. Yet the cancer was there—the cancer of liberties, franchises and immunities—the historic inheritance of the French system.

Arthur Young wrote that the poverty in the villages was indescribable. An English countryman would have compared it to agricultural conditions in the tenth century. As for taxation, when it was a question of privilege, there were infinite ways of escaping penalties or receiving favours, but when it was a question of the people, particularly the peasants, there was unmitigated rigour and harshness. For example, in 1767, the Duc de Choiseul attempted to stamp out the multitude of beggars who wandered from village to village and dragged on an intolerable life of despair and degradation. The stronger were sent to the galleys, the weaker to concentration camps. Over fifty thousand were rounded up by the police. They disturbed the sweetness of life, they must be spirited away, they spoiled the laughter in the gardens.

This we have come to believe is the true picture, or at least the important part of the picture, and with a superiority that relies on ignorance fully as much as it does upon documents, we pride ourselves on the "strange prejudices we are apt to take regarding foreigners." Yet Dr. Edward Rigby, an Englishman, travelling for the first time in France in July of 1789, wrote with great enthusiasm of the general appearance of the people and their apparent happiness. He described little parties sitting at their doors, some of the men smoking, some playing cards in the open air, and others spinning cotton. "Everything we see bears the mark of industry, and all the people seem happy."

Dr. Rigby was an agriculturist as well as a scientist. Where then does truth lie? With Arthur Young or Edward Rigby? It is simpler to accept Young's picture. A happy people does not rise in revolution—True. And yet neither does a people of scarecrows and spectres send their nobles and upper bourgeoise to deliberate in an Assembly on theoretical constitutions and obtain bread by speeches. The countless incidents and illustrations compiled by scholars and emphasised by political writers according to their views, whether traditionalist or revolutionist, remain a sort of "tasteless dregs" unless they are filled with the moral and intellectual ferment that produced the phenomenon of revolution. And nowhere did that phenomenon take more positive form than at the home of the first prince of the blood in the Palais Royal.

As for Philippe himself, a number of things happened to him while his naval career was running its brief course. He had been appointed Grand Master of the Masonic Lodge of France in 1771. He went up in a balloon, he went down in a mine, he made horse racing popular in France, he developed a severe case of anglomania, and he commercialised the gardens and courtyard of the Palais Royal which developed into a colossal centre of gambling and prostitution, thus inadvertently making him not High Admiral of France but Grand Pimp of the Kingdom.

CHAPTER X

BALLOONS

PHILIPPE can claim to be the world's first royal aviator, which is exactly what he intended to be. Going up in balloons was becoming popular in France. People were eager to subscribe to the expenses of any attempt. Philippe followed the development of this conquest of the air with great interest. When the first aviators, Pilâtre de Rozier and the Marquis d'Arlandes set off in a balloon on November 21st, 1783, he was there to watch them rise from the ground. Then, leaping on a horse, he followed the course of the balloon at full gallop, and when twenty minutes later they came down in a field some distance away, he was the first to cheer their exploit. Verses appeared saying that the English might have conquered the sea but the French had conquered the air. A whole flock of toy balloons rose into the French skies, some of them laden with such inflammable stuff that the police had to issue regulations concerning them.

Philippe was among the most enthusiastic followers of this new pursuit. In January, 1784, he commissioned the Robert brothers to build a balloon of the very latest type. It was fifty-two feet long, ending in two hemispheres of thirty feet on diameter. The rubber globe was covered with the strongest silk. The difficult problem was to steer it. This was to be accomplished by two wings of silk, one used as a rudder and one as a sail. The cost of this superb machine was about forty thousand livres, and Philippe looked forward to flying across the Channel and descending among his English friends.

An account written shortly afterwards describes the exploit in glowing terms. The ascent was made from the park at St. Cloud. An immense crowd assembled on July 15th, 1784, to witness the adventure, those in the back, says the historian Montjoie, shouting to those in front to kneel down so they could see the departure of this "superb machine." The wives of the Robert brothers hung on to the ropes until the great moment came. "Within three minutes the spectators lost sight of it. It rose to such a height that the voyagers not only lost sight of the earth but felt themselves borne into a region very different from what they had just left. Suddenly, although the weather was calm, they were enveloped in a thick vapour, an impetuous wind turned the balloon around three times, and the travellers abandoned all hope of being able to steer their ship—thick clouds gathered below them, seeming to prevent their return to earth. They were rapidly borne upwards to the surface of the sea of clouds. Then the heat of the sun caused the balloon to swell in an alarming manner. The Duc de Chartres judged that it would be foolish to risk further dangers. In order to descend, he imagined the thing to do was to empty the balloon of part of the gas which kept it above the clouds. Accidentally he tore a hole, some seven or eight feet across, in the silk which enclosed it. The gas escaped "*brusquement*" and the balloon descended very rapidly but none of the aviators was injured. The speed with which the balloon came down," added Montjoie, "made the Paris public accuse the Duke of cowardice. But this judgment was not just—his conduct on this occasion was more a proof of prudence than cowardice." It is a naïve little story and only one more evidence that once the public has been accustomed to laugh at any one it would consider itself abused if it could not repeat the diversion.

The balloon had in fact remained in the air for three quarters of an hour. It was one of the Roberts who had exclaimed, "Monseigneur, we are lost!" Philippe, who was enjoying the exciting journey, was perfectly calm, as he had been on the deck of the *Saint Esprit*.

"There must be something to be done about it," he said.

"There is," said Robert, "puncture the balloon."

"Where?"

"Anywhere."

As they came down they threw out ballast, and their landing was so gentle that only one of six full bottles which were in the basket was broken.

Philippe's *sang-froid* on this occasion is attested even by his severest critics. It is true that the flight had fallen far short of what he had hoped and predicted. That mere fact was enough to make the public invent stories of cowardice. He never made another flight. The Roberts tried again the following September and managed to stay up over six hours, and on January 7th

Blanchard flew across the Channel from Dover to the forest of Guines.

It is a strange irony that made the two days of action in Philippe's life into bywords in the mouths of idlers.

CHAPTER XI

GRAND MASTER

THE honour that Philippe acquired with the title of Grand Master is important because it linked his name with the forces that were thrusting into the future with an urge to improve the state of society and a benevolence of design which concealed the revolutionary tendencies underneath. Society decays from the top. Philippe as Grand Master is a curiously appropriate figure-head. He was elected in 1771, succeeding the Comte de Clermont, and his most noteworthy act as Grand Master was the suppression of the Grand Lodge of France[1] which was replaced by the Grand Orient. This change according to the masonic authority Papus (Dr. Gerard Encausse) was in favour of the revolutionary tendencies of French masonry. "Victorious rebels thus founded the Grand Orient of France." So a contemporary Mason is able to write, "It is not excessive to say that the masonic revolution of 1773 was the prelude and the precursor of the Revolution of 1789."

---

[1] A great deal has been written about Franc Masonry in the eighteenth century, and for those who are anxious to know the details, organisation and influence of the Lodges the books mentioned below will prove helpful.

L'Amiable — Une Loge Maconnique d'Avant, 1789. La R. L. les Neuf Soeurs, Paris, 1879. G. Bord: *La Franc Maconnerie en France,* Paris, 1908. J. J. Monnier: *De l'Influence attribuée aux philosophers, aux Francs Macons et aux illumines, sur la Revolution de France,* Paris, 1822.

The Origins of Freemasonry, Chap. V. Nesta Webster: *Secret Societies and Subversive Movements.* R. T. Gould: *History of Freemasonry.*

Talleyrand gives "as a curiosity" the acceptance of Philippe:

"In the year of great light 1772, third day of the Moon of Jiar, fifth day of the second month of the Masonic Year 5772, and since the birth of the Messiah, fifth day of April, 1772. In virtue of the proclamation made in the Grand Lodge, assembled on the twenty-fourth day of the fourth month of the Masonic year 5771, by the very high, very mighty and very excellent Prince H.S.H. Louise-Philippe Joseph d'Orléans, Duc de Chartres, prince of the blood, as Grand Master of all the regular lodges of France. And of that of the sovereign council of the emperors of the East and of the West, sublime mother lodge of Scotland, on the twenty-sixth moon of Elul 1771, as sovereign Grand Master of all the councils, chapters and lodges of the great orb of France: an office which the aforesaid S.H. has willingly accepted for love of the royal art, and in order to concentrate under a single authority all the masonic operations. In witness thereof, the aforesaid S.H. has appended his name to the report of acceptance."

Briefly it can be said that Masonry was in harmony with the new humanitarianism. "The origin and the reason whence, where and why the brotherhood of Freemasonry came into existence is, according to Masonic scholars, veiled in the mists of contradictory theories without any facts for their foundations." But the nature of Masonry at the time when Philippe signed his acceptance is lost in no mists whatever. A new spirit was permeating the lodges of France, a spirit that some English masons looked upon with abhorrence. John Robinson, an English Mason, has made astonishing statements in his book which he called *Proofs of a Conspiracy against all the Religions and Governments of Europe* carried on in the Secret meetings of the Free Masons, Illuminati and Reading Societies. He sought to prove that the new spirit was subversive and destructive of all the true principles of Masonry. In fact, the lodges were the early counterparts of the Jacobin clubs. He argued that only through such superb organisation is it possible to explain the apparently spontaneous outbursts of the Revolution, the uniformity of opinion and the effective opposition to counter revolution. France in 1789 counted more than two thousand lodges affiliated to the Grand Orient. The number of adepts was more than one hundred thousand. "The first events of 1789 were only Masonry in action."

French Masonry had been responsible for the *Encyclopedia* and its rapid dissemination throughout France. Behind it lay the idea of an intellectual revolution organised with studied care and by no means the result of haphazard outbursts of isolated geniuses. "The philosophers of 1770-1789 organised their terror no less surely than the Jacobins of 1793—but instead of the guillotine they used "l'infamie," or public condemnation, which in the provincial societies and reading circles and masonic lodges was a regular procedure of inquest, discussion, judgment and execution, that is to say condemnation to public infamy."

Most of the illustrious men of the time were Masons—d'Alembert, Diderot, Helvetius, Condorcet, to name only a few of those whose writings prepared the way for the Revolution. The lodge called the Nine Sisters numbered such famous men as Franklin and Voltaire among its members. Mirabeau was a Mason and traced out a plan of reforms for "brothers of the higher grade" which included many of the measures that he advocated later in the National Assembly. Lafayette was a Mason, and Freemasonry later claimed the "supreme honour of giving to humanity" his famous declaration of rights which formed the preamble to the constitution.

In the Army there were twenty-five lodges. The president might be, often was, a private, the colonel a mere delegate. The whole movement was symptomatic. How can you hope to uphold a system which your philosphy denies and your hope ridicules? Even the King, the Count d'Artois and Monsieur were secretly initiated. But Philippe himself, in spite of the prestige of his position, appears to have exercised little authority in the movement. His name lent the prestige that his character lacked. Yet admitting his apathetic leadership of the Grand Orient, it still remains significant that he was the nominal head of the most powerful group which was actively engaged in organising the Revolution: it still remains evident that he was consciously or unconsciously in the power of that invisible hand which seemed to be creating all the events; and which, declared the Marquis de Luchet, "had for its aim the domination of the world through a series of calamities of which the end is lost in the darkness of time like unto those subterranean fires of which the insatiable activity devours the bowels of the earth and which escape into the air by violent and devastating explosions." [1]

[1] This extraordinary prophecy was made by the Marquis de Luchet, in an *Essai sur la Secte des Illuminées* (ed. 1792).

CHAPTER XII

AN ARCHITECT OF RUINS

THE most important event in Philippe's life after the sudden end to his naval career was his speculation in the Palais Royal. His gambling and his extravagance had plunged him so deeply into debt that his income of 800,000 livres was entirely mortgaged from 1776-1780. There was no chance of increasing that income until the death of his father, or more particularly the death of his father-in-law. Something had to be done if he was to avoid a bankruptcy which would have serious consequences for the treasury as well as for the House of Orléans.

There is a passage in Suetonius which Philippe's enthusiastic haters were fond of quoting. It refers to Caligula, who like the Duke of Orléans " established a place of prostitution in his palace. He had little isolated chambers constructed which he had furnished with the same magnificence as his own apartments, and he destined them to be meeting-places for the citizens and courtesans." This is not far off the mark. But to satisfy the idle talk of the Parisians it was said that this new centre of gaiety and pleasure was a great drawing card for foreigners, which was true; that it stimulated industry and commerce, which was questionable as the industry was chiefly prostitution and the commerce was gambling. Moreover, it was rumoured that the Duc de Chartres had been ruined at the Court by his sympathies with the people, and that he had chosen this way of regaining his fortune at the same time as contributing to the gaiety of nations. And as the people of the Palais Royal, like the people anywhere, were eager to believe the truth is what they want, these rumours were to form the precarious foundations of a new popularity and turn this centre of extravagance into a political forum. The machinery would soon be there. Among the shops, brothels, cafés, gaming houses, threatres and music halls not least important were the printing presses, from which came the pamphlets in thousands as well as the daily and weekly news-sheets that were the uneasy barometers of public feeling. The mere fact that they were produced in the Palais Royal under the patronage of a prince of the blood gave them a stamp of security. It was known, for example, that there was bitterness and hatred between Philippe and Marie Antoinette, and the defamatory filth, the insinuation and libels which every cheap ink worm squirted on to paper and broadcast from the precincts of the Palais Royal could be sure of the semi-official, even if unacknowledged protection of the name of Orléans. Often the printing was not only acknowledged: it was sought after. Rivarol wrote at the beginning of 1789 that the Duke of Orléans sent the Duc de Biron to ask him to publish a pamphlet that should be called the Dilapidations of the Court, and that he refused the offer with disdain and said, " Send your lackey to Mirabeau, add a few hundred louis and your commission will be done."

Mme de Genlis takes the credit of saving Philippe from bankruptcy. As a matter of fact, the idea of speculating with the beautiful gardens of the Palais Royal, where society was used to stroll in the evening, first occurred to the Marquis Ducrest, her brother, who proposed it to Philippe during one of the many hectic conversations which sought a way out of his financial chaos. But before such a plan could even be thought of seriously it was necessary to persuade Philippe's father to cede the palace to him at once, instead of waiting until the indefinite date of his death. Without the guarantee of ownership no banker would advance the capital for the work. Ducrest, who had the enthusiasm of a company promoter, approached the old Duke of Orléans and carried all before him with surprising ease. The final papers were signed on January 1st, 1781, and by June 12th the plans of the architect Louis were approved. But not until the following August were the great trees cut down, while a curious crowd looked on, and the manager of the fashionable Café de Foy suggested gloomily to his clients that the end of the world was soon to be expected. As always, there was opposition. The proprietors of the houses overlooking the garden threatened an action to prevent their property being spoiled or cheapened by the erection of new buildings. They did more. They stirred up public opinion so that Philippe was hissed and booed in his own garden by the owners of push carts and wandering merchants who had become accustomed to treat the place as their own. There were seventy-two proprietors who considered themselves injured, and they used every possible means, legal or illegal, to stop it. A deputation waited on Philippe on April 6th, 1781, and after a very stormy meeting one of the injured gentlemen, M. de Boyer, cried, "We have two millions to fight you with, and we intend to fight." "I have four," said Philippe, who had taken a malicious pleasure in keeping the deputation waiting and had appeared in a dressing-gown and slippers. On August 30th, when the work had already begun, the infuriated proprietors did, in fact, bring an action in the Paris Court to prevent further progress —and lost their case. Philippe was in festive mood. When some one observed that the undertaking was so enormous that he would never be able to pay for all the necessary material, he laughed and said, "Yes, yes, for every one is throwing stones at me."

But as though this were not enough, Philippe gave the scandal-loving world of society another subject to talk about. On January 8th, 1782, the *Journal du Libraire Hardy* published something to satisfy the most exacting gossipmonger:

"The Duc de Chartres has just dismissed the governors and deputy governors appointed ten years before for his two sons, the Duc de Valois and the Duc de Montpensier, in order to hand over for the future the entire care of their education to the gentle Comtesse de Genlis, already the instructress of his daughters the two Princesses."

The news caused a tremendous sensation—a female

governor for the royal princes—unheard of. It was
an intrigue of the first water. The Duc de Chartres
was the dupe of the Genlis. Monstrous impertinence.
"The example set by the Duc de Chartres ought never
to find any great number of imitators," commented
Hardy in his Journal. Poems, songs, skits and epi-
grams came showering on the times. Part of the press
and society talked in rather heavy tones of the grave
consequences of this unprecedented move and shook
solemn heads in dismay. What was Royalty coming
to? It would have been a constitutional crisis had
there been a constitution. Instead it was a crisis of
etiquette, which is almost as strict and tyrannical as
most constitutions. Royalty had made an unexpected
move—a false move—a shocking innovation com-
promising its own dignity, and as always the public
gloated and leered and praised its own virtues while
censoring others. Garat wrote that people talk for a
day or two about a battle and then an opera makes
them forget it, but that a month after Mme de
Genlis's appointment it was still the chief subject of
conversation.

The "gentle countess" had left her own account of
it in her mémoires. Philippe, she wrote, came one
evening as usual between seven and eight o'clock to
visit her at Bellechasse, where she had already installed
herself as governess of the Princesses. He was very
agitated. He said at once that he must find a new
governor for his sons, that the present one, M. Bernard,
would make them into shop boys. He wanted advice.
Mme de Genlis mentioned several possible names.

Philippe turned them down at once. Then she laughed and said, "Well, why not me?"

Philippe grew serious. "Why not?" he said.

"I saw the possibility of something quite out of the common," she wrote afterwards. "Something famous, and I hoped that it might be possible for it to be realised. I told him my thoughts quite frankly. M. le Duc de Chartres seemed charmed, and said to me, ' You shall be their gouverneur.'"

According to etiquette, Philippe had to consult the King concerning the change. Louis did not hide his displeasure. "Happily I have the Dauphin," he is reported to have said by Garat and Prud-homme, "the Comtesse d'Artois has her two children. You have the right to do what you please with yours."

Talleyrand wrote that Philippe's choice was merely the intention to appear peculiar and to emphasise his scorn of accepted usages. Yet this is scarcely explanation enough, nor can the gentle countess's charming account be accepted at its face value. It seems very probable that this extraordinary departure from tradition had other motives behind it, motives which indicate great love of power in Mme de Genlis and an unusual amount of paternal affection in Philippe. Three and a half years after this appointment, when Bellechasse had already assumed the air of a small college presided over by the omnipotent "governor," Paris was interested to learn of the mysterious arrival, in May, 1785, of two little girls from England who were to live with the royal children as companions in order that they should learn correct English. The idea, it was said, had originated with Mme de Genlis, and Philippe had written to London to an agent of his, a Mr. Forth, formerly secretary to the British Ambassador in Paris, asking him to send him a pretty little English girl five or six years old after having had her vaccinated. Mr. Forth does not seem to have thought the request a strange one. Shortly afterwards he gave the child he had chosen into the charge of a horse-dealer who was crossing to Paris. "I have the honour," he wrote, "to send your Serene Highness the prettiest mare and the prettiest little girl in England."

Mme de Genlis named the little girl Pamela. However, this was not enough, wrote the Duchesse de Gonstant. "We looked for a family name, and that of Seymour was chosen and made known." Another little girl, named Hermine, two years younger, arrived shortly afterwards and was received into Bellechasse as one of the family (Fortunée Elizabeth Hermine de Compton, afterwards Madame Collard).

A great deal of mystery surrounds the origin of these two little girls. No birth certificates have ever been found. There was a highly improbable and romantic story that Pamela was the natural daughter of an English working-girl named Mary Sims, who was seduced by a French sea captain named Brixey and taken to Newfoundland, where she was delivered of a child. Later she returned to England, became a washerwoman at Christchurch, where Forth saw her and offered to pay her a sum of money if she would part with her daughter. The poor English working-girl is supposed to have welcomed this suggestion with, of course, suitable tears and sentimental sighs among the soapsuds. Thereafter Mary Sims discreetly disappears among the dirty linen of history and Pamela approaches the coast of France as beautiful as a Monday morning, in the arms of the jovial horse-dealer. The fact that this account was given years later in her marriage contract on December 27th, 1792, proves nothing whatever and does little more than to further the mystery. For the Tournais register gives her father's name as Beckley instead of Brixey, her birthplace London instead of Newfoundland, and states that she was about nineteen years old.

There were, however, other and more credible explanations of the mystery. On May 27th, 1785, the well-informed *Correspondance secrète* reported that both the children were the natural daughters of Mme de Genlis who had been brought up under fictitious names "These young ladies believed themselves orphans, when suddenly they have found their parents." Grimm's correspondence is no less clear, and certainly it was true that Pamela Seymour, destined to be the tragic bride of Lord Edward Fitzgerald, had a singular Orléans likeness in her beautiful dark eyes. And Horace Walpole remarked when he saw her years later in London that "Mme de Genlis had educated her to be very like herself in the face." Lord Edward Fitzgerald himself gave quite a different explanation of the mystery to his mother, the Duchess of Leinster. According to him, Pamela was a natural child of one of the Seymours. Yet in spite of these various and not too ingenious attempts to represent her as an English bastard, she was generally accepted and treated as the natural child of Philippe and Mme de Genlis. If this is true, and knowledge of the characters seems to make it probable even though documentary evidence is lacking, it would explain Mme de Genlis's position at Bellechasse as governor of the royal children even more clearly than the thousand-and-odd songs of the day, and it indicates that there was some method in Philippe's eccentricities, improbable though it appears.

A quality which never can be taken from him, solemnly declared M. du Boscq de Beaumont, one of his critics, is that of having been an excellent father. Certainly in all his correspondence, and in those moments when he is with his children, he becomes very human, even tender in his manner, as though the self-consciousness and timidity of his nature had vanished in affection.

.   .   .   .   .   .

But to return from Bellechasse to the Palais Royal. The construction of the new buildings and arcades took two and a half years. Philippe threw himself into the work with a restless tenacity that would not accept delay or defeat. They made fun of him at Court. "We don't see our cousin any more since he has become a shopkeeper," remarked the Count d'Artois. Mysterious placards with "Rue d'Ouessant," "Rue Saint Esprit," were found nailed on trees and arcades. Stories of his lust for money reached fantastic proportions. There is one told by Michelet in his famous history of the Revolution, that he was so greedy after gold that he tried experiments with black magic and necromancy in order to make it artificially. Among the necessary ingredients of one experiment was a human skeleton which had been a certain number of years in the earth. Among the famous dead it was discovered that Pascal exactly fulfilled the conditions. The guardians of St. Etienne were bribed, and poor Pascal was delivered and then dissolved in the crucibles of the Palais Royal. Philippe would have enjoyed that story. Actually, when the money was lacking in 1789 to complete the vast place, he resorted not to black magic, but to sound sense. He sold two hundred of his three hundred horses to the Queen and the Count d'Artois; he economised in every possible way; he dismissed many servants in order to pay his creditors; and the servants immediately joined the opposition which the defeated proprietors were still fostering. Finally, by January 1st, 1785, the work was completed. "This enchanting place," wrote a visitor, "is a small luxurious city in a big one. One could call it the capital of Paris. You find everything there."

In spite of attempts to ridicule the new Palais Royal, it was a tremendous success. The speculation exceeded Philippe's wildest hopes. Some idea of it can be had by imagining the Piazza St. Marco at Venice, but instead of the bare stone paving, a garden with trees. These trees, thirty years old, were planted a year before the work was completed, and immediately changed the whole atmosphere of the place. The public had grumbled because it had been excluded from the gardens. Now it found a new garden suddenly restored to it with a great number of yet unknown but alluring attractions in addition. Even the proprietor of the Café Foy smiled again. The Palais Royal became the fashion. You could not hope to know what was going on in town unless you strolled through its arcades or under its trees at least once a day. The great speculation became the centre of thousands of smaller speculations. Café owners, theatrical managers, shopkeepers, club proprietors, aristocratic gamblers, tumbled over each other to stake a claim in the place. The latest novelty, the newest marionette show, paid exorbitant prices for a booth, a theatre, or a room. The *Journal de l'Almanach du Palais Royal* kept you informed of the various sights and pleasures of the great bazaar. It gave the police more to do than all the other parts of the city together. It became the nerve centre of Parisian life. In the evening the walks and cafés were thronged with gay crowds that drifted from one part to another according to their tastes and their rank. Gambling clubs, theatres, vanity shows, brothels, wineshops claimed their habitués. There was a *Salon des Arts* and a political club which met at the Café du Caveau. There was a Club des Américains frequented by the many young aristocrats who had fought with Washington, Rochambeau and Lafayette in America. There was an Olympic Club to which ladies were admitted, and which was Masonic—not sporting, as it sounds.

The rents of this new world amounted to 550,000 livres, and it is interesting to know that most of the insurance was carried in London. With this increase Philippe's income amounted to the immense sum of four million, six hundred thousand livres, and made him the richest man in the Kingdom of France. In terms of present-day money it would be equal to about three million dollars, or six hundred thousand pounds; but in terms of present-day power it must be trebled, so that in order to form an idea of Philippe's financial position you must consider him as having had what to-day would correspond to an income of nine million dollars, or one million, eight hundred thousand pounds. The extent of his landed estates alone covered the extent of three departments of the kingdom. Beside his forests, agricultural lands, harbour and canal rights in various parts of the Kingdom, this new enterprise gave him a direct connection with a large portion of the people of the capital.

Yet although the enterprise was successful, it had in fact a very mixed effect upon his reputation. The Court and a large number of aristocrats looked upon it with envy which they mixed with disdain and not a little fear at the notoriety and increased power it gave to the House of Orléans. On the other hand, the riff-raff began to forget their limericks about naval battles and look upon Philippe as their patron and protector. Two events helped to make this division

[1] Lafayette wrote: "His fortune was enormous and was to amount at the death of his father to 12 millions a year." This is undoubtedly exaggerated, but an analysis of the Orléans fortune printed in 1791 gives an idea how immense and how widely spread it was. The active was estimated at the enormous sum of 117,976,946 livres, the passive at 67,611,258 livres.

deeper. On November 18th, 1785, the old Duke of Orléans died, and Philippe became head of the family and assumed the august title. More important still, on November 20th, 1787, he entered public life by leading the opposition to the King in favour of the Parliament of Paris and was promptly exiled to Villers Cotterets for his action. This dramatic moment was the prelude to the Revolution. It was evidence that men were prepared to build an opposition around the name of Orléans. From now on the innumerable crowds that thronged the gardens and the arcades became the sinister chorus of a quickening drama.

CHAPTER XIII

ENGLISH INTERLUDE

" JE m'en fous," Philippe shouted at some one who had drawn his attention to one of the numerous libels on himself which appeared in great quantities after the Battle of Ushant. And as far back as 1779, the editor of the *Correspondance Secrète* remarked that it was deplorable to see this Prince take so little care of his reputation that even his partisans are forced to abandon him and to believe the evil which is spread about him.

In fact Philippe had become a bad habit with the scandalmongers and pamphleteers. Many of them lived in the French colony of London and invented their stories from the wildest rumours. It was understood among this backbiting community that Philippe was common copy. Anything curious, exotic, caddish or in bad taste could be attributed to him. He would do nothing about it—nothing, that is to say, which would inconvenience them in the noble art of muck raking.

His indifference hid a contradictory nature. He leaned towards the advanced principles of his day without having either the imaginative or emotional driving power to direct them. The bleak heights of power only charmed him when he was comfortably seated in the valleys below. And yet he had a better and more favoured view of them than most men. He could not conceive of happiness in terms of work, but must look for it in terms of eccentricity.

He had been attracted to English customs and English ways long before he crossed the Channel. He was the first to set the fashion in adopting the English frock coat, in doing away with powdered hair, in wearing shoes instead of slippers, in driving his own coach. He had made racing popular in France, and initiated what was known as the reign of the jockeys. Anglomania became the rage among a cosmopolitan society which lived a life of its own apart from the people, and considered politics, wars and other unpleasant things as existing in a different and inferior world.[1]

Englishmen had always been welcome at the Palais Royal. Their singularity was considered charming, and their independence and spirit of opposition were especially in harmony with the Orléans spirit. But with the Court it was different. Louis XVI. and Marie Antoinette deplored the importation of this foreign influence. It became one more source of irritation, and as usual Philippe did nothing to make it less.

In fact, before the close of the American War, he commissioned his friend Forth to find him a *pied-à-terre* in London—"a place where I can arrive from Paris whenever I want to and don't have to render an account of my conduct to any one whomsoever." It was the request of a prince who longed to be an inde-

---

[1] Even during the American War, Horace Walpole wrote many letters to Paris and received many answers from his French friends.

pendent gentleman. He wanted some stables, of course—enough for a dozen horses, though he did not mind which part of town the *pied-à-terre* might be in. In August, 1782, Forth rented for him No. 35 Portland Place, at 350 louis a year. The owners wanted him to take the house furnished, but Philippe wrote to Forth that he preferred to choose his own furniture— "because I believe that furniture as well as women must be chosen according to the whim of the moment." But except for this royal *bon mot*, he treated everything to do with the house with a care for detail and an accuracy which one of his biographers has termed bourgeoise, to distinguish it from a carelessness which is supposed to denote a princely taste. Forth offered to sublet part of the house himself, but Philippe wrote him that he was welcome to live there when he was in London, as a friend, without paying rent, and added, "Beside the satisfaction I will have in doing you this little service, I will be certain that my house is well taken care of."

He longed to get away from the intrigues of the Palais Royal, to arrange the new house exactly as it pleased him, to come and go as informally as he did from *Monceau*, his country house on the outskirts of Paris. Prevented by the Court from taking any part in the American War, his restlessness expended itself in plans for the future, in a hurried visit to Italy, in a thousand details concerning the Palais Royal.

The cessation of hostilities was finally proclaimed on February 4th, 1783. By the 8th of March, six months and a day before the Treaty of Versailles, the

cross-Channel ships resumed their daily service from
Calais and Dover, crowded with visitors from both
countries. Philippe reached London on May 4th,
under the name of the Comte de Joinville. His only
regret was to have missed some of the race meetings.
London charmed him, and he made himself particularly liked by his enthusiasm for everything
English. The London papers with their quaint
snobbery and self-satisfaction followed his movements
and reported his sayings. Three days after his arrival
he was reported as intending to honour the King's
Theatre with his presence for Madame Theodore's
benefit.

The following day he was present at a debate in
the House of Commons, that "very agreeable coffee
house," where "members came in in their greatcoats
and with boots and spurs. It is not at all uncommon
to see a member lying stretched out on one of the
benches while others are speaking. Some crack
nuts ; others eat oranges or whatever else is in
season."

On coming out Philippe remarked, "I would be
very happy to sit among you if I were English. I
admire a government where the authority is the will
of all." His position in France as titular head of the
opposition to the Court drew him towards the Whigs.
But other things besides mere politics and principles
had quite as much Whig influence upon him. Society
was a vast gambling house, and whenever two or three
were gathered together the dice or the cards were sure
to be in their midst. "The gaming at White's," wrote

Walpole, "is worthy of the decline of our Empire."
"Gambling," wrote Sir George Trevelyan, "in all its
forms was rather a profession than a pastime to the
leaders of the London world." Not only at White's
and Brooks's did Philippe meet the leaders of that
world, "the dandies and the rakes who filled their
pockets from the Exchequer and emptied them over
the hazard table": he was also a welcome visitor at
that great Whig stronghold—Newmarket. A few
days after his visit to the House, the *Morning Herald*
of May 12th contained the following news: "Yesterday the Duc de Chartres and his suite set out for
Newmarket, where he saw the running of the great
Claret Stakes of 200 guineas, the owner of the second
horse to receive two hogsheads of Claret." This must
have been one of the most popular races of the season
at a time when a large part of Society sailed from
race course to club and from club to country house
upon a vast sea of claret.

"The face of the Duc de Chartres," wrote the gossip
reporter, "is so completely overspread with a *rosy
tinge* that the *lilies* of his ancestry may be said to
receive not the least countenance from him." Like
others around him, Philippe gambled and drank
claret. One of his French biographers tries to heap
scorn upon him by declaring that he adopted the
manners of the clubmen of London and the republicans
of the United States of America. He was a deep player
at the tables, but not deeper than many a plunger of
the time. When he was losing he was invariably gay
and courteous. It was a point of honour and etiquette

to lose gracefully—but when he was winning he would become brusque and curt in his manner and his speech, a peculiarity which became a habit with him later during the Revolution. It was inevitable that he should meet Charles James Fox in this world of gambling, racing and drinking. This "phenomenon of the age" had established his reputation as the greatest plunger that London had ever known. His losses were said to exceed £140,000. Upon one occasion Philippe lent him a sum of money to help him out of a particularly disastrous run of luck. The amount is unknown and the generosity is not distinguished, as Fox appeared to be able to wheedle money out of anybody, including the waiters at Brooks's and the chairmen who waited outside the door.

Philippe made many other acquaintances and friends, among them the Prince of Wales, who was causing the King, his father, acute distress by his extravagant behaviour. He thus found himself among the group that formed the opposition to George III. Yet it was not a political move as much as a temperamental coincidence. He loved novelty, he hated the tyranny of formal etiquette, and he found it exhilarating to be in London, where the influence of men predominated (as it always has) rather than in Paris, where (at least before the Revolution) women ruled. Not that he abandoned his love affairs. On the contrary, a gossip writer with more than customary reticence remarked upon the meeting of a certain royal visitor with a lady at Ranleigh who was already in royal favour, and it is not unlikely that he referred

to Philippe and Grace Dalrymple Elliot, a beautiful
Scotch girl who was welcome at Carlton House and
who passed from one royal lover to another with no
difficulty whatever.

The English public was further informed that his
royal highness contemplated settling in England with
his family and Mme de Genlis, so that his children
could be educated as English children, which naturally
was the best method. Philippe's happiness at living
as an independent gentleman flattered every one. It
was easy for society to be pleased with French royalty
when it appeared in such an affable form and with so
much money to spend. "It is hoped," wrote the
Morning Herald, when Philippe had paid a second
visit to Newmarket with the Duke of Dorset,
"it is hoped that his Gallic Royal Highness will be
more successful this visit than his former one,
when, it is said, his Grace was eased on that day of
8,000 guineas."

Everything about Philippe was noticed and commented upon. The *gold auricular pendants* of some of
his suite came in for good-natured laughter, and under
the title of "Masquerade Intelligence," the *Morning
Herald* of May 22nd had the following extraordinary
paragraph:

"The set of coat-buttons lately worn by the Duc
de Chartres, and which gave offence to several
ladies on account of the *subjects* exhibited on them,
are now laid aside. Some of the *maids of honour* who
have examined them very minutely have declared

that the most exceptionable button in the set consisted alone of a little *frolicksome device* from the
antique, and that they would have no scruples to have
an *apron* worked after the pattern."

But perhaps the best comment, both on Philippe
and on the London that he was enjoying, is in the
same paper on May 23rd. "What is intelligence
from the *beau monde*," wrote a sprightly reporter,
"unless Monsieur le Duc de Chartres takes the lead
in it?

"—His Grace's exterior is now sufficiently
known—his interior graces are as near as can be in
exact conformity.

"—His Grace's favourite studies, or rather amuse-
ments, for such by long habit they have become, are
in Natural History.

"—In attentive investigation of that noble animal
the horse he is supposed to exceed M. Buffon. In his
analysis of the vintage even Dr. Armstrong is said to
be left behind.

"—The two English gentlemen who from simi-
larity of study are now principally about His Grace
in the quality of *arbiter deliciarium* are Lord Grosvenor
and Lord Surrey.

"—His Grace is not only very anti-Gallican in his
appearance, but in his manners is also very exempt
from the peculiarities of the Frenchmen.

"—He is said to have no rage for enterprise and
adventure, and as to any imputation of vivacious
animal spirits, romantic gallantry to the fair sex and

113   H

conversational loquacity His Grace is certainly to be acquitted on the evidence of Lady Jersey, Mrs. Crew, etc. etc."

He appears to have been an excellent unofficial ambassador for his country, so excellent, indeed, that the official ambassador, le Comte d'Adhémar, writing to the Foreign Minister on March 6th, remarked that he wished other visitors could be as gracious. Montmorin was silent. His part was with the Court, and the Court disliked Philippe's Anglomania and distrusted his friendship with his English friends. The idea that he could be in any sense an ambassador was inadmissible. Moreover, "our cousins across the Channel" were held in no very high esteem by the French Court, who viewed the conquests of their hereditary enemy with distrust and considered the manners of a people who were guilty of regicide extremely barbarous. John Andrews, an English traveller, has an interesting comment regarding this. "When he boasted of the political liberty of his country, a Frenchman retorted that the English had beheaded Charles I., but that the French gloried in having always maintained an inviolable attachment to their kings; a fidelity, a respect, which no excess or severity on his part has ever shaken." This was written in 1785—which only emphasises how quickly earthquakes can come.

Philippe's first visit was not a long one. There are glimpses of him at dinners and masquerades. There was the inevitable talk about the English weather solemnly reported, for the spring of '83 was an exceptionally bad one and he was importuned not to think there was always so much rain and dampness in England. On May 30th, the *Herald* reported that Philippe and the Duke of Cumberland had returned from the Derby, and a week later he left for Paris, having taken his leave of George III. and his many acquaintances and friends.

But by March 21st of the following year (1784) he was back in London again. One of his horses—Cantator —ran in the Derby and the papers were full of quips and whimseys about His Gallican Highness.

The indefatigable *Morning Herald* reported on Sunday, May 5th: "The Prince of Wales and the Duc de Chartres dismounted yesterday afternoon in Hyde Park and walked arm in arm for some time in Kensington Gardens. The Prince appearing rather *pale* and *Mons le Duc* very *rubified*, it was observed that the Heir of Great Britain had taken up with the *lilies of France* and resigned the *rose of England* to the Prince of Bourbon!

"How uncommonly *rosy*," cries one, "appears the Duc de Chartres!" "He should be called the Duke of Burgundy," observes a second . . . A third subjoins, "His Highness has just returned from a *betting post* and is *flush* with success."[1]

The following day the same paper contained a comment of a more serious nature. "His Royal Highness the Duc de Chartres is commanded by the Grand Monarque to return to Paris immediately.

---

[1] The rubified appearance of Philippe's countenance, which was an endless source of heavy witticisms was not, as many people believed, due to claret, but to a kind of eczema which took this unpleasant form.

The Court of Versailles, it is said, are really afraid that the Gallic Prince should imbibe certain Whig principles during the present political struggle in England which may not be easily shaken off."

This conjecture, flattering as it was to the English reader, was somewhat mistaken. Philippe's hurried return was due to his financial troubles and the pressing need to raise money. Yet the general sense of the London paper was true. Philippe had witnessed the riotous elections of '84, he had listened to the passionate debates in the House of Commons, he had seen the surging mobs and heard the cries of "Fox for ever," and his friendship with the Prince of Wales had linked his name with the opposition and the democratic ideas connected with it. Yet the French Ambassador reported to Louis XVI. that his connections with the Prince of Wales did not lead him to share in his excesses. "The bearing of M. le Comte de Joinville in London is in every respect excellent." He had dined at the French Embassy with Fox himself on the very evening of his triumph at the Westminster poles. There is no doubt that every move was reported and that this anglomania, mixing politics with pleasure, was highly unpopular at Versailles.

During 1785 he made three different trips to England. During one of them, in April, he was painted by Reynolds. The famous painter was then at the height of his popularity among the fashionable world and the portrait of Philippe is in his best manner. It remains a precious witness to Philippe's appearance at thirty-eight years of age, He wears the uniform of colonel-general of Huzzars. His figure is heavy but well poised and his head is held high with a natural dignity. The face is typically Bourbon, the expression has a false seriousness about it. The mouth is sensuous, the eyes are large and handsome, the feeling about the face is inconclusive, as though satiety had taken the place of beauty and a certain disgust of life lurked in the background. Reynolds charged him two hundred and fifty guineas which was considered dear by Philippe's friends in England. However, he paid without remonstrance and had a number of engravings of the portrait made. The following year he presented the original to his friend the Prince of Wales and the first gentleman of Europe hung it on the walls of Carlton House.

During these visits to London the papers gave their usual attention to the royal visitor, and even suggested that he might be future ambassador. It did not matter that his chief pleasures in England were racing and gambling. It did not matter that he was quite as anxious to lead in a Derby winner as to follow the mysterious workings of that world of unrest which was pushing him with relentless and increasing power into prominence. It is not difficult to exaggerate a fear until it becomes a formidable fact, and the Court at Versailles was beginning to fear the spirit of opposition that was taking form about the rubified features of the Duke of Orléans.

How justified was this fear? How villainous was Philippe under this surface of an amiable roué? The evidence must be examined.

It is certain that he deposited and invested large sums of money in England during his many visits. A letter from ᵢGeneral Montesquiou to a friend in London, written on November 15th, 1793—that is to say, eight months and five days after Philippe's death—mentions the sum of ten or twelve millions (about half a million pounds) besides a large number of diamonds.

Joseph Lavalle writing in 1816 on the *Factions of the Revolution* made the following statement, for which he offers no proof beyond his own words. " M. d'Orléans often went to England. M. d'Orléans was very fond of England, though not of the English. The wisdom of their laws mattered very little to him but the liberty of London mattered to him a great deal. This apparent love of the Duke of Orléans for the English was in the end the cause of all the calumnies against England with which the leaders of the different factions influenced public credulity so as to throw on the policy of that nation the excesses of which they alone were guilty."

Montjoie, a passionate supporter of Louis XVI. and the old *régime*, was more specific, though he, too, makes his assertions from hearsay. "During his visits to London the Duke of Orléans personally, and by means of his agent in Holland, made fresh loans of money in England. He attached to his interest Lord Stanhope and Dr. Price. These two men were the most important members of a society calling itself The Revolution Society. D'Orléans also knew how to interest all that party known as the opposition in his cause. Fox, one

118

of the oracles of this party, was throughout attached to Orléans, and still is to his family (this was written in 1797) he is the declared protector of all the Frenchmen who belong to the faction of the Prince."

More mysterious figures than Fox come into the picture. It was stated by Mr. Gordon Hills that Jewish information had been supplied to him showing that a certain high initiate of International Masonry, named Falk, had been in touch with the Duke of Orléans in London. This mysterious figure is suggested as one of the sources from which came that almost mystical "l'or de Pitt" that was supposed to be at the bottom of every riot in the Revolution.

This damaging evidence seeks to prove that Philippe was, even at this time, an arch-conspirator, that his investment of funds in England had ulterior motives behind it, and that his designs were deep-laid and diabolical. But it is quite as probable that the origin of the flight of Orléans capital to London was as natural as the flight of capital to-day from any disturbed country in Europe to London or New York. Moreover, before 1787, there is not the slightest evidence that Philippe ever made plans for a Revolution in order to revenge himself for the slights and insults, imagined or real, which he had received from the Court. Nor can he be considered as an ambitious ringleader urging his followers on to unjustifiable acts of slander or open rebellion. Like most weak characters, it is true, his vanity expressed itself in revenge when it was thwarted. His position and his wealth made him a magnet for men who were far more able intriguers.

A party was already forming around him. Mirabeau's remark, "There was an Orléanist party but the Duke did not belong to it himself," is a revealing comment. Until 1787, Philippe had taken no part in public life. His first appearance was immensely important. It marks the opening of the great conspiracy. It opens the Revolution.

CHAPTER XIV

THE ISSUE IS JOINED

So much blame can be laid at the feet of Louis XVI. for the qualities that he lacked, qualities of decision, strength and vision, that it is too easy to forget the majesty and greatness of the French throne, which, until 1789, united in itself the soul of a state of twenty-six million people, the most powerful, cultured and prosperous in the world. By general consent the fair land of France was recognised as the first and most excellent in Christendom, "as well by reason of its dignity and power as of the absolute authority of him who governs it." Thus spoke a Venetian ambassador. He who governed it was the redresser of abuses, the guardian of the right, the protector of the weak, the great almoner, the universal refuge. Such was the sentimental abstract conception of the throne. And of Louis XVI., Bailly wrote in his memoirs: "Despotism had no place in the King's character; he never desired anything but the happiness of his people, this was the only means that could be employed to influence him—a less kind-hearted king, clever ministers, and there would have been no revolution."

Yet as the year 1787 approached the agitation of men's minds became greater and the anxiety of the state of the national finances hastened a crisis which the current stories of court extravagances and royal pensions only exasperated.

Moreover, Calonne, the newly appointed Minister of Finance, was disliked by the people of Paris who considered him a spendthrift and distrusted his pose of a grand seigneur assuring every one that things were getting better and better. He was supposed to be intimate with the Queen and to have encouraged her extravagances, which in the public mind were assuming astronomical figures. It is unfortunate that in times of public nervousness news that is believed is more important than news that is true—in fact the beliefs form themselves into a reality which has to be faced by whatever authority exists. Calonne was quite incapable of facing it. Actually the Queen was far from being intimate with him. She hated him. Moreover, he was not a spendthrift but a vain, practical man whose main idea was to raise money to meet the deficit by taxing the privileged classes. This naturally was unpopular with the Parliaments which were strongholds of privilege. Calonne then proposed a convocation of Notables to solve the difficulties, and the King willingly consented.

On February 22nd, 1787, one hundred and forty-four exalted personages gathered at Versailles and listened to Calonne's opening speech with grave misgivings. He made a very bad impression by misreporting the amount of the deficit and talking about his own virtues. During the following weeks he was attacked by various members, including Lafayette, and the King was forced to dismiss him on April 8th. It seems extraordinary to reflect now that the deficit was estimated at under seven million pounds in a country which had been able to finance the American war to the extent of forty-four millions. But it was not the amount itself as much as the system by which money was raised that caused the confusion.

Two of Calonne's projects for taxation remained— one a tax on landed property and the other a stamp tax on contracts and patents. Both of these proposals were taken up by Calonne's successor, the Archbishop of Toulouse, Loménie de Brienne, who assumed control of the finances in May. The events that followed centred entirely on the problem of taxation. The Parliament refused to register the two taxes. The King held a *lit de Justice* (Aug. 6th) and registered them by force. The Parliament protested (Aug. 7th) and was exiled to Troyes on August 15th. Public opinion was all on the side of the Parliament, which became the champion of opposition to the Court. The King, wrote Beaulieu, was overwhelmed with petitions from *all classes of citizens*, with remonstrances from all the Courts of the realm in favour of his Parliament of Paris. The Queen was greeted with cries of "Mme Deficit!" Public business was at a standstill and the King was forced to capitulate and recall the Parliament, which was received with wild enthusiasm by the people, who imagined, quite wrongly, that these long gowned and bewigged gentlemen were overflowing with public benevolence.

Brienne was now forced to concoct another scheme to meet the deficit and pay for current expenses. He proposed a loan of four hundred and twenty millions, and in order to register the edict the King summoned Parliament on November 19th, 1787. Throughout the summer and autumn the Convocation of the Estates General was fiercely talked about. As early as July 16th, the Abbé Sabatier, an intimate friend of the Duke of Orléans had suggested it. Since then the idea had gained in strength. It seemed to be merely a question of the date.

Meanwhile until that time should come, the Parliament appeared to be the centre of popular opposition to the crown and the guardian of national interest. It alone could object to the registration of the laws, and the meeting on November 19th had a peculiar sense of expectation and excitement about it.

The Duke of Orléans and other princes of the blood were present. Philippe had not distinguished himself in the Notables although he had been appointed to preside over one of the committees. He had scandalized the people of Paris by spending a great part of his time hunting. On one occasion the *correspondence secrète* reported that he was so far carried away by the ardour of the chase that he followed the quarry through the Faubourg Montmartre, the Place Vendôme and the Rue St. Honoré as far as the Place Louis XV., not without having overturned and wounded several people. The sight of a deer bounding through the Place Vendôme and along to Rue St. Honoré, hotly pursued by Philippe and his friends, is certainly among the more picturesque flights of a reporter's fancy. Talleyrand mentions a hunt which ended in "the ditches of the Faubourg St. Antoine—to the great scandal of the Parisians."

But however apathetic Philippe may have appeared towards the Notables his interest in this meeting of Parliament was unfeigned and extremely personal. If the loan was voted he, as a great capitalist, would be one of the most affected. Moreover, it appeared to those who were intimate with him—to Mme de Genlis, to Ducrest her brother and Philippe's chancellor—that here was a golden opportunity to attack the Court and win an easy popularity.

The King announced that he had come to consult his Parliament on two great acts of administration and legislation. He left the explanation of these acts to his Keeper of the Seals, the Marquis de Lamoignon, but he took occasion to remonstrate upon the action of the Parliament in opposing registration of laws, and he employed a tone of authority "which," remarked Talleyrand, "being affected and not even sustained during the little time he spoke, served only to make perceptible by its variations the hesitations of his character."

The Marquis de Lamoignon followed his royal master—but with no hesitations or variations. He upheld the absolute power of the King. He attacked the proposal for the Estates General and intimated that it depended entirely on the royal will. He then turned to the various advantages which were to be expected from the proposed loan of four hundred millions, and at the same time drew the attention of the members of the Parliament to the King's personal economies and other virtuous qualities which should serve as an example. The discussion was then thrown open, and during the next seven hours various opinions were expressed for and against the edict. The most eloquent speakers, M. d'Espresméil, Sabatier and Freteau, urged the King not to be deceived by his members and to convoke the Estates General in order to regain the public faith and give the nation a means of reforming its affairs.

At the end of this long debate when the votes upon the edict were about to be collected the King made the following pronouncement: "I ordain that the edict be transcribed on the register of my Parliament to be executed according to its form and tenor."

This was exactly the turn in events that the opposition had been waiting for. The King had scarcely finished when the Duke of Orléans rose and said, with a clear and steady voice: "If the King holds a royal session of Parliament the votes ought to be collected and counted . . . if it is a *lit de justice* he imposes silence upon us." He paused. The King answered that it was a royal session. "Sir," continued the Duke of Orléans, "allow me to lay at your feet the illegality of your orders."

The effect was overwhelming, the principles of authority which surrounded the King, the traditional ideas of centuries of procedure were suddenly upset, and by the first prince of the blood. The King's orders were declared illegal a moment after he had pronounced them in a session of his Parliament.

"The whole history of the monarchy offers nothing

like it. Princes of the blood had not been seen to resist the power of the King with arms in the hands: they had never been seen to try to impose constitutional hurts to his authority."

The King was embarrassed at this unexpected opposition. He said quickly, "Yes, it is legal because I wish it," and proceeded to have the edict registered. Then, obviously disturbed, he rose and withdrew from the Court.

Immediately afterwards the Parliament registered the protest in its minutes, thus making the edict invalid and the gesture of revolt complete. The protest was in these words:

"The Court considering the illegality of what has just passed at the royal session in which the votes were not counted in the manner prescribed by the ordinances so that, in short, the deliberation was not completed— declares that it wishes it to be understood as taking no part in the transcription ordered to be made on the registers, of the edict regarding the establishment of loans, gradual and successive for the years 1788, 1789, 1790, 1791, 1792, and puts off the deliberation of other matters until the next meeting."

This declaration announced to all France that the Duke of Orléans had put himself at the head of the opposition. As a political gesture it was vigorous and well-managed. The moment was excellently chosen, and even Talleyrand, looking back on an unparalleled career of successful intrigue, could grudgingly admit that "the Duke of Orléans had carried off all the honour of this day, and it must be acknowledged that

127

all had been planned and conducted with great skill by him and his friends."

Outside the court-room the news-hawkers broadcast the result of the extraordinary session to enthusiastic crowds. Philippe had become a symbol of resistence to privilege and arbitrary power. People besieged the doors and carried him in triumph to his coach, shouting his name and praising his courage. It is not unlikely that he scoffed at the idea of his own leadership afterwards. "Do not imagine that I made this stand against the King," he said to Brissot, "in order to serve a people I despise (the people of the Palais Royal) or a body of which I make no account (the Parliament), but that I was indignant at a man treating me with so much insolence." Moreover, it is not improbable that the real reason behind it was a question of money. He had heavily subscribed to a previous government loan which would fall in value if the new loan were voted. Even accepting this explanation of his bitterest enemies the historical fact remains that he had suddenly become a symbol of popular hope. The King was aware of this, and to prevent further mischief he had determined to ignore the incident. He had been informed that the opposition had been planned at the Palais Royal during the previous evening, and although he resented his cousin's intrusion, he wisely decided not to make a double victory for his opponents by punishing them. Most of the decisions that the King made were both wise and tolerant but almost all of them suffered the fate of this one and died an apathetic death. Marie Antoinette, however, was determined that Philippe should suffer. The royal dignity had been compromised. She demanded his exile and the arrest of the two councillors. When the King hesitated, she insisted. When various courtiers ventured to suggest that the King was right and that such a punishment would only increase popular sympathy for the Duke of Orléans, she insisted still more emphatically. The King yielded and a triple *lettre de cachet* was made out the following day against Freteau, Sabatier and the Duke of Orléans. Freteau was imprisoned in the citadel of Doullens, Sabatier in the prison of Mont Saint Michel, and the Duke of Orléans was exiled to his country estate of Villers Cotterets. Marie Antoinette had humiliated her hated enemy once more. But she had also played into his hands, or rather, into the hands of his councillors.

It was, as the King had foreseen, an easy way to make him into a popular martyr. Moreover, the situation was made worse by the use of a great display of military force on the day when the *lettres de cachet* were issued. Although the King regretted this he was powerless against Marie Antoinette's demands. The Queen, wrote Montjoie, never altered a resolution once she had taken it. Her stubbornness was building the royal scaffold.

CHAPTER XV

THE VILLAIN OF THE PIECE

THE success of Philippe's intervention was partly due to Mme de Genlis whose influence over him at this time was very great. In her position as governess of his children she lived in an apparent retirement at Bellechasse. But in reality "Bellechasse was the antechamber of the Palais Royal." The principal people in Philippe's service were responsible to her for their places. Sillery, her husband, was the Captain of his Guards; Ducrest, her brother, was his chancellor; Valence, her son-in-law, was his first equerry. Simon, his business manager, had been given his appointment by her influence. Her power extended so far that it is claimed by her biographers to have influenced his choice of a new mistress, Mme de Buffon, the young and pretty daughter-in-law of the great scientist. By a curious subtlety in feminine nature, Mme de Buffon "never tried to separate M. le Duc d'Orléans from Mme de Genlis, whom she looked up to as a superior woman capable of advising her well," and Mme de Genlis could regard with sure satisfaction the fact that, after 1787, the sport of collecting girls from the lowest quarters of Paris and throwing them naked and drunk into the park at Monceaux, ceased to be a ducal pastime. "From that time," wrote Mirabeau's friend, La Marck, "one ceased to see women at Monceaux and there never appeared any again."

But from the period of his exile to Villers Cotterets another influence began to make itself felt. Mme de Genlis wrote in her mémoires that at this time she had every reason to be discontented. "The Duke of Orléans made the strangest proposition to me. He told me that M. le Vicomte de Ségur had asked him for a post as *Secrétaire des Commandements* to the Duc de Chartres for M. Laclos, the author of the *Liaisons Dangereuses*. I was disconcerted. After a moment's silence I answered that if he gave that position to such a man, I would give up the education of his children the following day."

In spite of this threat Mme de Genlis did not resign, and Laclos was given the post of *Secrétaire des Commandements* to Philippe himself. Choderlos de Laclos was forty-seven years old, of Spanish origin, and a retired officer of engineers. He was better known as the author of a novel called *Liaisons Dangereuses* which had had an enormous success. "He had studied the politics of love because of his love of politics." From the moment of his appointment he became one of the most important people who influenced the Duke of Orléans. He was, in fact, from now on the soul of the Orléanist party.

Like Mme de Genlis, Laclos was a *parvenu* of the *petite noblesse*. These two recognised, understood and hated each other with all the cordiality possible between two intelligent intriguers fighting for control of a royal quarry: a control which promised the achieve-

ment of ambition and the rewards of unscrupulous
cleverness.

This man of forty-seven who had kept himself
swimming in the great world of society by a series of
light, inconsequential verses and a satirical and
crapulous novel, now entered upon his true career.
The people he had laughed at and exaggerated in his
book now became his tools and his partisans. His cold
demeanour, his energetic mind, his calculating eyes
understood the mannered simplicity, the "feeling"
and the culture of the "gouverneur." He had no use
for her literary taste which concealed a passion for
power under its remarkable display. She on her side
recognised and feared the power of action in her rival.
Her instinct told her that it was dangerous both for
Philippe and for herself. How dangerous was not yet
apparent. These boudoir conspirators, these theorists
and roués with their hate of the Queen and their endless
intrigues, make up an incongruous chorus at the
opening of the Revolution. "The women seated at their
toilets, plunged in the soft luxury of their boudoirs,
said, 'A revolution is a nice thing—let's have a
revolution. The people are the best in the world, the
King is a good King—everything will be splendid.'"

Pamphlets and broadsides were appearing by the
hundreds. People passed them from hand to hand at
the street corners. Lackeys handed them over garden
walls to other lackeys. Scandal, treason, and rumours
jostled each other in a sea of ink. Philippe's study in
the Palais Royal was full of them. Along the chimney-
piece stood a row of notices which Laclos had been

engaged in writing. These contained instructions about the coming election, which was the chief topic of conversation. For Philippe it was as much a personal as a political event. "One will soon be able to go to England without the King's permission," he exclaimed. But those about him looked nearer home. Their eyes were on Versailles. At Bellechasse, Mme de Genlis was holding those famous afternoon receptions during which, Barère, Pétion and Brissot exchanged their ideas, while at the Palais Royal her rival, Laclos, was being entertained by Mirabeau's ribald stories. Laclos had not forgotten the Duke's remark when he had complained that his brevet as secretary had not yet arrived. Philippe had laughed and remarked, "They say that you are not a gentleman." Such a jibe to one walking along the outskirts of society would not be easily forgotten or forgiven. Now he had his brevet and he intended to work this princely goldmine until it yielded him something that paid for insults. Decent people, he reflected, if any such exist, are only lambs in the midst of a pack of tigers. It is better to be a tiger, because it is better to devour than to be devoured.

But he was "more like a spider than a tiger"—a spider in the Palais Royal spinning the web of discord, riot, and revolution out of the crowds in the dusty gardens and noisy archways below the great windows. Unknown, unscrupulous, and unafraid of the greatest designs, he preferred to work behind the mask of his royal master. He could listen to the applause and the shouting and feel the thrill of power without ever facing the fickleness of the crowd. "This fellow,

Laclos," wrote Dumont, who met him at Mirabeau's house, "attached to the Duke of Orléans, was a sombre, taciturn man, with the face and look of a conspirator, but so close in his speech that I scarcely spoke to him although I met him several times." Characteristically it was not Laclos but Brissot, the eager and volatile journalist, who outlined the famous conspiracy during 1787, in a series of letters to Ducrest. The main ideas were these: It must be ostensibly a plot in favour of the people. The Constitution would be the slogan. The head of the party must be the House of Orléans. It would appeal to the historical and sentimental feelings of the people.

Sillery talked about it openly. He was certain that the weak Louis XVI. would have to put the power into other hands during the tempest. He believed, moreover, that the Duke of Orléans in matters of high importance would reveal qualities which would make him dear to the French people as he was dear to his intimates. This is an important testimony coming from the historian Droz, who would have heard a great deal of oral tradition. The ideology of the moment was to be adopted and a certain largesse to the people given with plenty of publicity. The outline of the plot was fairly classic. The throne was not to be upset. That was manifestly impossible even to consider in 1787, or in fact in 1789. But the Duke of Orléans could be made Lieutenant-General of the Kingdom with power over the finances and the ministers. There was precedent for that.

Such was the main outline of the great conspiracy.

How far did Philippe concur in it? How active was he in pushing it forward? Nothing is easier to denounce than an abortive plot, nobody is easier to malign than a conspirator who fails. Yet Philippe's character belies the *rôle* of the great conspirator. His hatred of the Court, particularly of the Queen, was the exasperation of a weak nature. In the schemes of Laclos, in the advice of Mme de Genlis he saw a way of striking back, to rid himself of the perpetual hindrance that the Court had been to his whims, his desires and his activities. One more blow to his pride and his vanity had recently been added to the rest. The Queen had interfered to prevent a proposed marriage between his daughter Mlle d'Orléans and the Duc d'Angoulême. He had reached a state of mind where everything that would serve for revenge was welcome. "The Duke of Orléans," wrote Malouet, "had his own intrigue quite apart. His personal aim was vengeance (on the Court, and particularly on the Queen). The aim of his council was not democracy but profit."

Yet one must walk carefully among this intrigue and counter intrigue. The Court blamed all the growing unrest and most of the disorder on this conspiracy. Royalist writers, from the contemporary Montjoie to those of the present day, have emphasised the villainy in order to proclaim the supreme virtues of monarchy, which since the time of Plato have been very open to question. Mme de Staël was nearer to truth when she wrote, "An entire people is not put in motion by such means (as the Orléans fortune). The great error of the people of the Court has always been to seek in some little detail the cause of feelings expressed by the entire nation." Yet the little details are not to be ignored.

All over France the resistance to the royal will was felt and applauded. The deep current of life was flowing in the direction of democracy. The war for American independence had given it irresistible strength. Those who opposed it were amazingly impotent; those who would have used it for new despotisms could only stain it with blood; and those who dreamed of controlling it were swept on by a power that was stronger than any individual will.

It was on this stream so strong and beautiful with human hope that the Duke of Orléans was to be carried to popularity. But under the strength and the beauty lay intrigue, lust for power, hatred, cynicism, corruption and selfishness. Supported by Laclos, and at times by almost every figure in the revolutionary calendar, the name of d'Orléans echoes loudly, but withal hollowly, from the opening act of the revolution.

CHAPTER XVI

LETTRE DE CACHET

ON November 20th, the day after the meeting of Parliament, the Baron de Breteuil, the minister specially entrusted with the delivery of *lettres de cachet*, had come to notify the Duke of Orléans that he was ordered by the King to go immediately to Villers Cotterets in the canton of Aisne and remain there at His Majesty's command. It was a delicate mission. Breteuil had acquired a large part of his fortune under the protection of the House of Orléans, and Philippe was not the person to lighten his embarrassment. When the ducal coach was called and Philippe was was about to drive away, Breteuil made as though to get in beside him. "What are you doing, sir?" "I have orders to accompany you in person, your Highness," replied Breteuil. "Get up behind then," said Philippe, slamming the door. Breteuil shrugged his shoulders, got into another coach and, armed with the *lettre de cachet*, followed his royal prisoner at a discreet distance.

This was one of the last *lettres de cachet* ever delivered. Originally intended to convey the royal decrees, they had been used for two centuries as a weapon to control, intimidate, exile and imprison any one displeasing to the King or to any member of the nobility who could obtain the signature of the Secretary of State.   The cause was often imaginary and trumped up to cover personal vengeance. Their exact counterpart has, of course, reappeared in Europe with the dictator states. Russia, Germany and Italy employ just such methods to deal with those who stray from political orthodoxy. Often in France under the old *régime*, the *lettre de cachet* was used for personal reasons. The head of a noble family found it singularly effective in keeping unruly members of his household in order. The old Marquis de Mirabeau, for example, lightened the burden of his marriage, which he described as "one long renal colic," by shutting his wife in a convent, and his son, the future orator, in the state prison. This bad business was bitterly attacked by Lafayette, and was finally done away with by the National Assembly.

Philippe's exile at Villers Cotterets lasted just under five months and on the whole can only be treated as ludicrous, if it did not form a part of that chain of events which roused his hate of the Queen to an unnatural passion. By exiling him the Court had given him a cause of discontent which with a little firmness and dignity he could have made into an imposing symbol of arbitrary persecution. Instead he behaved petulantly and ignominiously. During the first days of his exile he was visited by many distinguished people, among them the Prince de Conti and the Duc de Bourbon. His wife, the Duchess of Orléans, and her sister, the Princesse de Lamballe, came to Villers Cotterets to try to lighten the rigours of a luxurious exile. Their efforts were fruitless. The Baron de Benseval, who broods over the old *régime* with so much affectionate knowledge, wrote that Philippe's longing for Paris was so great that he sacrificed this chance to add to his reputation, by writing letters to the King beseeching him to remove the *lettre de cachet*. He sent Ségur to Benseval begging him to intervene. The Princesse de Lamballe was even sent to plead with the Queen. To complete the farce, Philippe was as madly in love with Madame de Buffon as a boy of sixteen, and the need to see her outweighed all others. This young and pretty person was the exact opposite of Laclos. Talleyrand declared that her disinterestedness and her extreme devotion won her the indulgence of all who knew her. During Philippe's exile she came every week to Nauteuil, half-way from Paris, where he went to see her.

But if Philippe's behaviour was incongruous, that of the Parliament was both effective and adequate. On November 21st, they resolved to ask the King "to recall to his presence the august prince whom he had removed and to return to the Court two members whose zeal alone had dictated their opinions."

In his reply the King referred to the fact that he had already said that he would convoke the Estates General before 1792, but that he could not admit the declaration of the Parliament that the edict was illegal.

On January 11th, the Parliament addressed another protest to the King. The tone of this letter was contained in one sentence: "If the Duke of Orléans is guilty, we are all guilty."

The King replied that he had nothing to add to what he had already imparted to his Parliament.

"Every one," he added, "is interested in the conservation of public order, and public order depends essentially upon the maintenance of my authority."

The Parliament took up the challenge of this absolutism and expressed its ideas on law and authority in menacing terms. "It is not one of Your Majesty's functions personally to condemn criminals. This painful and dangerous function can only be exercised by the King through his judges . . . We dare to demand the judgment or the liberty of the Duke of Orléans and the two magistrates imprisoned by your orders."

Again the King returned an evasive answer. The Parliament of Toulouse rallied to Philippe's cause and added its protest, followed by all the other provincial parliaments. Finally the Paris Parliament printed a long exposition of its legal rights in a pamphlet which had a prodigious success. The result of this war of words was once more a capitulation by the King and a removal of the *lettres de cachet* from the three members of royal displeasure. But in Philippe's case there was a provision calculated to irritate him at the same time as freeing him. The *Correspondance Secrète* reported: "It is confirmed that one of the conditions that the Duke of Orléans's exile should be cancelled is that this prince should make a long journey to anywhere except England. To the well-founded reasons the King may have for preventing him from breathing British air, there is *they say* to be added the entreaty of George III. who, wishing to maintain the footsteps of the Prince of

Wales on the path of order and modesty, has begged his most gracious Majesty not to allow his friends in Paris to approach."

The writer of this correspondence is unknown and "they say" is one of those historical authorities to be treated both with respect and circumspection.

What remains, however, is this: The Spirit of Revenge was only further aggravated by this condition.

"From the moment of his exile," wrote Ferrière, who was no Orléanist, "people forgot the debauches, the avarice, the swindling of the Duke. The people only saw an illustrious victim of arbitrary power, and weary of the instability of the government, of the gross ignorance of the ministers, seeing no end to their own misery, they turned their eyes towards the Duke as towards the only man capable of protecting their rights. The Duke himself animated by violent hatred of the Queen, to whom he attributed his exile, let himself be led into any project that could further his vengeance; but guided by his own timid nature, he kept hidden behind the intrigues that men plotted under cover of his name."

CHAPTER XVII

FAMINE AND ELECTION

THE winter of 1788-89 was one of the bitterest of the century. The Seine was frozen. There was a food shortage in Paris. The suffering among the peasants and the poorer classes in the cities was appalling. In this crisis the clergy and the nobles acted with the greatest generosity. Gifts of money, soup kitchens, and free meals were organised all over the country. In Paris the Duke and Duchess of Orléans were conspicuous by their charitable activities. Philippe's chancellor published a notice in the *Journal de Paris* saying that one thousand pounds of bread would be given away daily to the needy (Dec. 20th, 1788), while the crisis lasted. The Court professed to see dark designs behind this charity—a bidding for popularity which could be used against them. There *is* a darkness in this terrible winter when cold and famine were competing with hope and idealism during the preparations for the election to Estates. But it was not a darkness deliberately created. "All the efforts of the clergy and the nobles could not keep pace with the immense mass of indigence, which was swelled by the confluence of dissolute and abandoned characters from every part of France. These wretches assembled round the throne, like the sea-birds round the wreck which are the harbingers of death to the sinking mariner, and already appeared in fearful numbers in the streets on the occasion of the slightest tumult. They were all in a state of destitution, and for the most part owed their life to the charity of the ecclesiastics whom they afterwards massacred in cold blood in the prison of Carmes."

There were frequent bread riots. "Bread," wrote a contemporary, "was the potent lever by which the people were roused to action." The real authors of the scarcity were the farmers and the bakers, who conceived their interest to be in keeping up the price of bread. Unconsciously they played into the hands of men like Laclos, and undoubtedly the crisis was used to increase the Orléans hold on the popular imagination. But it was not only lack of bread that was rousing the people, nor the feebleness of the weak creatures at the Court, nor the hidden intrigues of Laclos. France was teeming with sudden intellectual activity. Thought, like an electric current, was alive with a new brilliance. Misfortune and weakness seemed only to stand in stronger silhouette. As the spring approached the famine spread, and the government struggled desperately but vainly to relieve the distress. Private individuals added prodigal gifts. The Bishop of Chartres contributed twelve thousand francs, an unknown wealthy man forty thousand francs. The Archbishop of Paris sold all his plate to feed the poor and contracted debts arising to four hundred thousand livres. Convents and charitable institutions fed thousands of people for months at a time. What bread there was had a musty taste. Long lines of people waited for scanty rations "fit for dogs to eat." In the midst of such a national disaster the election took place.

It was one of the strangest elections in history. A general restlessness possessed every one. There was an abandon and an intemperance in words and in ideas. "One might have thought," wrote Ferrière, a deputy of the nobility, "that the people had awakened from a long enchantment suddenly to record their faculties of talking and thinking. The real traits of the new development were especially to be seen in the cafés of the Palais Royal. There was a curiosity to hear everything, to know everything, a need of self-communication that unceasingly drew a crowd of citizens there. One would come armed with a constitution which he proclaimed confidently must be considered by the Estates. Others declared against the Ministers, the Nobles, the Priests, preparing thus the general opinion necessary."

The Keeper of the Seals, M. Barentin, had ordered all the royal agents "not to permit themselves to seek to determine the choice of the voters, or to take any steps that may tend to impede the voting." This impartial and ideally liberal attitude of the King was far from being followed by the other parties. Philippe's part in the election was a very active one. Laclos drew up a list of seventeen articles comprising a set of instructions for the electorate of his domains. They upheld the following principles: individual liberty, liberty of the press, privacy of letters, respect for property, taxation by consent, periodical recurrence of the Estates General, ministerial responsibility, establishment of a budget, equality of taxes, reform of the civil and criminal legislation, responsibility of public magistrates. Other measures in this energetic pamphlet of Laclos dealt with the importance of the *Tiers d'Etat* or Commons and the abolition of certain feudal and seignioral rights. It was a document in tune with the spirit of the time and it rallied a large body of opinion to the Palais Royal and the Duke of Orléans. One article, No. 12, seemed extraordinarily advanced. "We demand the establishment of divorce as the only method of avoiding the unhappiness and the scandal of ill-assorted unions." People said at once that it was put in by Philippe so that he could get rid of the Duchess of Orléans and marry Mme de Genlis; but this attack on the indissolubility of marriage, which seemed then such a revolutionary measure, was a veiled attack on Marie Antoinette. Her increasing unpopularity might be made to rouse public feeling to such a point as to compel her to withdraw from her position as Queen. The means of withdrawing would be already established.

Mme de Genlis persuaded Philippe that the instructions of Laclos needed editing. They were too blunt and, from her point of view, they reflected too much favour upon her rival. Accordingly the Abbé Siéyès, who had recently gained a great reputation by several political pamphlets, was enlisted to modify or improve the instructions. Instead of which he composed an entirely new pamphlet called "Plan de délibérations à prendre dans les Assemblées de bailliage." Siéyès's

K

connection with the Orléanists was limited to this pamphlet which, together with the instructions of Laclos, had a wide influence in determining the tone of the *cahiers* or list of grievances and reforms which the deputies brought with them to the Estates.

"Siéyès," wrote Bourrienne, "had written on his countenance 'give me money.'" He is one of the metaphysical wind-bags of the Revolution, "quite ready to abandon his constitutional dreams for a good round sum." But on this occasion he could combine the two and find good pay for dreams.

"Profound?" exclaimed Talleyrand. "Yes, he is a cavity—a perfect cavity, so to speak!"

The election took place in the country between March 10-16, and in Paris between April 15-25. The Duke of Orléans was elected by the Nobles of three constitutions—Villers Cotterets, Crespy-en-Valois and Paris. He chose to sit for Crespy, which seems strange at first, as Paris was the source of all his power. But Laclos had judged that it would appear another popular gesture towards the people. It gave him greater freedom of action, and the course that that action was to take became suddenly and tragically revealed a few days before the opening of the Estates General.

CHAPTER XVIII

APRIL 28TH, 1789

"AN event," wrote Ferrières, "to which not enough attention has been given was the Reveillon riot."

On April 28th, 1789, a crowd of five or six thousand men and women, many of them workers, under the pretext that a certain rich manufacturer named M. Reveillon had treated them badly, marched on his house, followed by an immense crowd of people who seemed to have come from the four quarters of Paris. His house was sacked, his shops and warehouse pillaged and destroyed. The police were unable to disperse the crowd, and several companies of the French and Swiss Guards, with a train of artillery, were called out. "One cannot recall having seen in Paris such a military force directed against the inhabitants. Parisians have never had much love for troops in war kit among them. The former government had until now taken the precaution not to afford them such a spectacle. Several blank volleys were fired, which only called forth curses and jeers from the crowd. The troops were then ordered to load their rifles with shot and to fire on the populace. A great number of people were killed, and the massacre went on for a long time."

Beaulieu, who recounts this, was present himself, and his comments are illuminating. "Many people," he wrote, "have considered this riot as the effect of discontent among the workers. The author of this work believes he can prove the contrary. He ran to the Faubourg St. Antoine the moment that the rumour of the riot reached the centre of Paris; he saw most of it, and made many inquiries from peaceful citizens of the neighbourhood. He discovered that the paper manufacturer, Reveillon, was a very honest man who paid his workers well; and even supposing that there had been cause for discontent concerning salaries they were free to go and work elsewhere and work in that trade was plentiful.

Moreover, the crowd of rioters was by no means composed of workers in the Reveillon factory. Almost all of them were drunk, and they certainly were not driven to it by despair. It appears evident that the riot was the result of some abominable plot which should serve as a trial for future operations.

Some inquiries were begun by the Parliament and then suddenly and mysteriously dropped. Was it because the Parliament was afraid of finding its late champion, the Duke of Orléans, at the bottom of it, and preferred to compromise the authority of the King rather than to expose some one whom they had supported in the past?"

One of the characteristics of every violent crisis of the Revolution is the sudden disappearance from the scene of the leaders. You see them before and hear their plans, you see them afterwards and hear their comments; but during the violent movements, the surging of the people through the streets, they have discreetly disappeared, and their responsibility can in many cases only be deduced by implication or by a knowledge of their characters. In the case of the Orléanist conspiracy this is especially true. So much of it took place behind shut doors, so little was written. Most of the references to it are in the memoirs of those who, like Lafayette, rose up to fight it, or of mere observers, like Montjoie, who erected it into the arch bogey of the Revolution.

Montjoie was another eye-witness of the riot, and though less trustworthy than Beaulieu, his account is interesting because Philippe can be seen for a moment in the tumult. "The ruffians who led the riot," he wrote, "went into the factories and workshops of the district and compelled the workmen to follow them against their will. They themselves were not Parisians, but were chiefly composed of ferocious-looking men from the south of France and Italy who had lately been in evidence about the streets of Paris and in the gardens of the Palais Royal." If this is true—and several memoirs of the time confirm the assertion—it is only one more evidence of the amazing inability of the Court and Government to deal with the most elemental police matters. A spontaneous rising is extremely rare and must necessarily be difficult to deal with, but a government which allows hairy brigands armed with clubs and dressed like the villains of cheap melodrama to wander about the streets of its capital and foment riots is more despicable than the conspirators who make use of such primitive methods to turn them out of office.

The crowd surged into the Rue Montreuil in the Faubourg St. Antoine, where Reveillon's house was already guarded by a few troops. The Duke of Orléans, on his way to the races at Vincennes, had chosen to drive through the Rue Montreuil. Seeing the crowd, he got out of his coach and talked with some of the men, slapping them on the back and saying, "Allons, mes enfants—de la paix: nous touchons au bonheur." The people cheered him, but did not disperse. He continued on his way and returned later, this time with the Duchess. Meanwhile more troops had been sent for. Three regiments of French and Swiss Guards were now concentrated about the house. When the Orléans coach was passing through the Rue Montreuil on its return journey, it opened a passage through the troops which gave the mob a chance of breaking through. The people cried, "Vive la maison d'Orléans!" Not until several hundred had been killed was the riot quelled. Reveillon's house was sacked. Numbers of rioters died of chemical poisoning, which they drank thinking it was wine; others died of the wine. The walls dripped blood, the pavement was covered with wounded and dying. "They died gaily," said an eye-witness. Most of them declared that they were mere onlookers. "It was not possibly to make them say anything else. There never was such an example of laconic humour, of such discretion." Apparently even the third degree was not able to make them say what Monjoie and the authorities wanted them to say—that they had been paid by the Duke of Orléans to raise the riot—because the punishment would be certain death. The prisons overflowed with them after they had been arrested. But only two workers were convicted and a woman with child. The woman was reprieved, and the men went to their execution like heroes, while a sympathetic crowd looked on at these precursors of a vast army of human beings who were destined to die by civil violence during the next four years.

There is every reason to believe that the whole affair was organised by the Orléanists. Talleyrand said quite clearly that Laclos had managed it. The Duke of Dorset, the British Ambassador in Paris, writing to the Duke of Leeds two days later, reported that the Duke of Orléans "has experienced repeated marks of popularity lately, and particularly on Tuesday last. As he was returning through the Faubourg St. Antoine the people frequently called out, ' Vive la maison d'Orléans! '" The sight of the livery of Orléans was enough to rouse the mob to enthusiasm. " Long live our father," they yelled. " Long live our King Orléans."

Chamfort and Mirabeau both admitted that the riot had been financed by the Duke of Orléans. Chamford was pleased with how little the experiment had cost: twelve francs a person was a miserable price to get killed for. Mirabeau declared that with a hundred louis you could make quite a nice riot.

The similar amount of money—twelve francs, in two pieces of six ecus each, in many cases wrapped up in envelopes—found on the rioters strengthened the conviction that the riot had been engineered by professional agitators. Moreover, not a single contemporary account shows any belief that it was a spontaneous rising of the workers against their employers. The only possible explanation of why Reveillon had been singled out for violence is that he had defeated the Orléanist candidate for the Estates General. It was then an election riot which probably went far beyond what Laclos had intended or Philippe had imagined. Not that they were particularly sorry. The violence served their cause admirably. The revolutionists, in fact, immediately spread the fantastic tale that the whole affair had been engineered by the Court in order to furnish an occasion for asserting its authority and firing on the people. The Court was often intolerably stupid, but it is difficult to believe that it could have deliberately destroyed its waning prestige by such a move—especially when you realise with astonishment that this rumour, fostered as it was in the Palais Royal, was readily believed. It spread through the faubourgs to vast numbers of people who were living in an eagerness of hope and a longing for better things. It made thousands of eyes turn in anxious perplexity towards this mysterious and bloody outburst in the Faubourg St. Antoine where, like a symbol of the old order of things, towered the Bastille.

CHAPTER XIX

THE FACTION GROWS

THE Reveillon Riot marks the beginning of what that brilliant writer Augustin Cochin calls the inconceivable tyranny of the Palais Royal. "This beautiful kingdom of France, so perfectly civilised, this generation so superior to our own in matters of taste, culture and politeness in the broad and ancient sense of the word, this century whose debris our own is now disputing, copying the last relics as clumsily as the barbarians copied imperial Rome, was plunged into the abyss—suddenly—in a few months—into blood and brutality under the stupid tyranny of the Jacobin caliban."

As the flood rises and the mist is whirled thicker in the revolutionary atmosphere, the form of the Duke of Orléans becomes more indistinct. Sometimes he assumes the legendary mantle of the genius of evil, at other times the wavering outlines of feebleness obscure his features. The initiates of the new cult revolve about him, worshipping not him but the impersonal and occult force which they have evoked without understanding and which will break them without effort as it has raised them up. "Everything is allowed to any one acting in favour of the Revolution," cried Collot d'Herbois. "In other words, men will demand of an act from now on, not is it good or bad, but is it revolutionary or not."

On May 4th, a week after the Reveillon riots, the gathering of the Estates General was celebrated by that gorgeous procession which seems now like the farewell of the old *régime* to its own pomp and pageantry. The following day Louis XVI. opened the session of the Estates in the magnificent *Salle des Menus Plaisirs*. On both days Philippe made himself conspicuous. In the procession he walked among the deputies instead of with the other princes of the blood. Moreover, he walked ahead of the order of the Nobles, so that he appeared to be among the ranks of the third estate. Cries of "Vive le Duc d'Orléans!" greeted him all along the route, while Marie Antoinette was received with a silence that throbbed with hostility.

Governeur Morris, who had recently arrived from America on business, and who viewed the scene "from a cramped position," noted in his journal that "the Duke of Orléans was received with cheers by the commons." In fact his popularity, carefully fostered by Laclos, who at last had his hands in the duke's coffers, seemed to be increasing every day. During the period between the opening of the Estates and the fall of the Bastille his activity is more evident than at any other time. Twice he was within reach of the supreme power of the Kingdom, the first time legally, the second time illegally, and both times he hastily retreated into obscurity.

The question of the reunion of the three orders gave him his first opportunity. Already his activities were suspect. It was said that he was intriguing Paris to arouse public opinion by bribery at the same time that he was assuring the Comte d'Artois that he would never unite with the Commons. On June 17th, however, he made it clear that he was in favour of union with the Commons. He spoke with apparent effort; the room was extremely hot, crowded and stuffy. A deputy named le Marquis de Montrevel called out, "Open the windows." Philippe, feeling faint, sat down. Friends crowded around him, offering him smelling salts, unbuttoning his coat and waistcoat, and finding to their surprise that he had on a great number of waistcoats, one of them being of stout leather, apparently as a protection against assassination.

His enemies jeered. Some said it proved that he was about to undertake some desperate act. In reality he was in danger of arrest—possibly of being murdered. The question of his arrest had already been raised in the King's Cabinet. The Court presumed that all the trouble came from him and his party. M. de Lamoignon, the former Keeper of the Seals, had not been afraid to venture such an opinion. It was opposed by Monsieur, the King's brother, and the King as usual remained uncertain and finally rejected the advice. "This explains the cause of the suicide of M. de Lamoignon, which took place then, and which no one suspected at the time." Certainly Philippe was informed of this intrigue against him through his numerous spies, and it explains the leather waistcoat as well as the suicide of M. de Lamoignon.

Philippe's motion for union was rejected, but on

the 24th he led 77 members of the nobility to join the third estate, an act of open revolt against the King's edict which had ordered them to deliberate separately.

"While these gentlemen were on their way to the Assembly," wrote Beaulieu, "the Duke of Orléans was applauded in a sort of delirium by the people about the hall."

Philippe put his head out of the window of his carriage and made some banal remarks deprecating the noise and evoking public happiness, which produced more cheers.

Three days later the rest of the nobility followed and the King capitulated once more. The Duke of Orléans was elected President of the National Assembly by 553 out of 869 votes.

This large majority alarmed the royalists, who saw in it only another proof of superiority of the Orléans faction. In reality it proved nothing of the kind. It proved simply that the commons saw in the figure of the Duke of Orléans a symbol of opposition to the Court and to absolutism. His name had been linked with the ideology of liberal reform which was popular at the moment, and in the first months of the revolution all the various groups and forces marched together under one banner without distinguishing the dividing lines which later became battlegrounds. For Laclos, Sillery, Ducrest and others of the Palais Royal Philippe's election doubtless would have been a step nearer to their goal, which was the destruction of social order and control of the kingdom. It would have made Philippe the practical head of the nation.

From there to the creation of the office of Lieutenant-General was a short step. Thus at the very opening of the Revolution the Orléanists seemed to have gathered to themselves the hope of a nation to cloak the workings of their own ambitions and destructive designs. The wreckers were marching in popular colours.

But they reckoned without their frontispiece.

Philippe's reply was characteristic. "If I believed," he said to the Assembly, "that I was able to fill the place to which you have elected me, I would accept it with joy; but, gentlemen, I would be unworthy of your goodness if I accepted it knowing well how little I am fitted for it. Accept, therefore, my refusal, gentlemen, and see in it only the indubitable proof that I will always sacrifice my personal interest to the good of the State."

Just as he stands ready to emerge into a distinct individual, for good or for evil, he sidesteps into the mists of rumour and secret meetings, and his name floats through the conversations and speculations like a bad omen.

An immense whispering campaign against the Queen was started from the Palais Royal. It was said that the troops which the Court had ordered to converge on Paris were the means by which Marie Antoinette would close the Estates, sack the Palais Royal and ruin the Parisians. Mirabeau declared loudly to all the deputies that if one wanted to be free a great change must be brought about at Court. The Duke of Orléans must be made Lieutenant-General of the Kingdom. He assured those who inquired whether the Duke of Orléans approved the project that that prince had answered him in a most friendly way about these matters.

One day, remarking on Mounier's attachment to the king and the monarchy, he burst out impatiently, "I want a king as much as you do. But what does it matter whether it be Louis XVI. or Louis XVII.?"

So once again the emphasis slips off Philippe on to those around him.

Mirabeau's activities as an Orléanist are wrapped in obscurity, but it seems certain that he had some hope at this time in the political fortunes of Philippe. His friend, la Marck, defends him from the charge of accepting money, but there is no doubt that he knocked at every political door and went in and out of most of them at one time or another. "I have seen him," wrote Mounier, "pass from the nocturnal committees held by the friends of the Duke of Orléans to those of the enthusiastic republicans, and from these secret conferences to the cabinets of the King's ministers, but if from the first months (of the Revolution) the ministers had consented to work with him he would have preferred to uphold the royal authority rather than ally himself with men he despised. His principles must not be judged by the numerous contradictions in his speeches and writings, where he said less what he thought than what happened to suit his interests under such and such circumstances. He often communicated his real opinions to me, and I have never known a man of more enlightened intellect, or more judicious political doctrines, of more venal character and of a more corrupt heart."

If Philippe's part in the National Assembly was limited to his refusal of the presidency, his friends at the Palais Royal lost no opportunity of keeping his name in the political limelight by exciting the passions and exasperating the feelings of the motley crowds that thronged the gardens. During the last week of June and the first two weeks of July there was a crescendo of fêtes, fireworks, speeches, harangues, disorders and distractions amounting to madness. According to the reports of a police agent, decent people no longer ventured into the courtyards or the gardens, where the bull-like face of St. Hurougue shouted at gaping crowds. There you could see strange sights. Men carrying banners with "Vive le Roi, Vive le Duc d'Orléans, Vive le Tiers d'État" inscribed on them. Frenzied orators shouted to pull down the chateau of Versailles, to declare the Duke of Orléans general-in-chief. From the Palais Royal went the mob that freed the soldiers of the French Guard imprisoned in the Abbaye for insubordination. "The Duke of Orléans orders that the gates of the gardens be left open all night," and the released troops were fêted in a wild orgy.

Moreover, a terrible and decisive force had entered the scene—"the mob of brigands which," wrote Rivarol "the Revolution and the gold of a great personage had attracted to Paris." Here was the great backing of the Orléanists. At Montrouge, a village near Paris, Laclos and others of the duke's party held their nocturnal meetings. They were different from the meetings of the already famous Breton Club, which was to develop into the conquering Jacobins. The Breton Club wanted power and publicity. The intriguers at Montrouge and the Palais Royal wanted locked doors, long cloaks and secrecy. The meetings were wrapped in a sinister and melodramatic silence. They would be mere play-acting, were it not for these lawless, hungry and ferocious bands of men and woman to work upon. Even from the windows of the Palais Royal money was thrown to the frantic crowds below. These were the people whose golden idol Philippe had for the moment become.

CHAPTER XX

JULY 14TH, 1789

ON July 11th Layafette wrote: "Amongst the persons who bring themselves most forward in the Revolution there are some whose views extend further than the establishment of a constitution. I am convinced that the Duke of Orléans, or at least the people who push him on, intend doing mischief. Some words have been repeated to me and some advances made. I was told yesterday that the head of the Duke of Orléans and my own were proscribed, that sinister projects were formed against me, as the only person capable of commanding an army; that the Duke of Orléans and I ought to take all measures in unison; that he should be my captain of guards, and that I should be his. I coldly replied that I only considered the Duke of Orléans as a private individual somewhat richer than myself, whose fate was not more important to the nation than that of any other members of the minority; that it was useless to form a party when we are with the whole nation, that it is necessary to do what is right without vexing ourselves by consequences and either build the edifice ourselves or bequeath materials to other men. But in the meantime I watch over the Duke of Orléans and shall perhaps be obliged to denounce at the same time the Comte d'Artois as a factious aristocrat and the Duke of Orléans as

factious by more popular means. All these plotters of
evil as well as the agents of despotism shall be disappointed by the force of circumstance."

Three days before the fall of the Bastille, therefore,
and one day before the serious rioting began, Lafayette
was approached by agents of the Duke of Orléans. If
(for a moment) he had favoured the intrigue it would
have succeeded. He was the idol of the respectable
part of the nation, of the vast majority of the bour-
geoisie, of the people of Paris. His enthusiasm for
liberty was fanatical, his honesty unimpeachable, his
popularity immense and his vanity unlimited. He was
not unaware of what was taking place at the Palais
Royal, and if there was one thing that he hated more
than the idea of absolute monarchy it was the idea of
a usurper whose methods would add violence and
corruption to absolutism. From the moment when he
became informed of the Orléanist intrigue he became
its fiercest opponent. He turned its two major attempts
at wrecking and destruction into triumphs for the
nation. The fall of the Bastille and the march on
Versailles were intended by the Orléanists to be the
signal for violent changes which should carry them
to power. In each case what Lafayette termed "the
force of circumstances" disappointed them, and the
event went far beyond their intentions. "In the first
case," Lafayette wrote, "the cause of the nation
triumphed, the Bastille was taken." And the king, by
coming to Paris and accepting the symbol of the
Revolution in the form of the red and blue cockade

(ironically enough the Orléanist colours) scotched the Orléanist attempt and helped to create the myth which has surrounded the rioting and murdering of July 14th ever since. In the second case, the march on Versailles, it was, according to the testimony of many who were present, only by Lafayette's presence that the lives of the royal family were saved from the mob which was organised and led by agents of the Palais Royal. Moreover, it was Lafayette who definitely killed Orléanism in its last attempt to remove the king by mass petition. The "massacre" of the Champ de Mars scattered it to the winds.

. . . . . .

There has been a lot of talk about the monopoly in grain affected by the agents of the Duke of Orléans at this time. Lafayette wrote that the famine in Paris was partly real and partly factitious, that it was the torment of the magistrates and the principal resource of intriguers and seditious people—among which he put the Orléanists first. "But when we consider the enormous amount of hoarding necessary to starve a country like France, one cannot believe that the faction of the Duke, no matter how powerful it was, could have brought it about." Possibly not; but there is no doubt whatever that the mob orators and agents of the Palais Royal seized on the country's misfortune and aggravated it by every possible means in their power, which was very considerable.

In fact, everything was playing into the hands of the conspiracy: the number of brigands in Paris had grown to alarming proportions. Wild bands of men wandered about the city attacking food shops, bakers' shops, wine shops, and spreading terror among peaceful citizens. Their numbers are estimated to have been between twenty and forty thousand. Even the lowest figure is sufficiently terrifying. The hot night echoed with their shouts and drunken singing. As the first rumour of a government crisis spread on July 11th a wave of hysteria seemed to sweep over the city from the centre of disorder, the Palais Royal, while at the Hôtel de Ville the distracted magistrates were striving frantically to cope with the crisis, and a citizen militia, the beginning of the national guard, was being formed to protect Paris from the brigands.

On the morning of the 12th the panic-mongers at the Palais Royal spread the news of Necker's dismissal and added that the Duke of Orléans had been thrown into the Bastille by order of the Court; the troops were closing in on the city; all was lost. "It would be difficult," wrote Montjoie, who was present, "to paint the picture that the Palais Royal presented on this stormy morning. Masses of people pushed and jostled each other. Sometimes there was a silence of consternation; sometimes you heard a sombre and menacing noise like the booming of the sea under a violent tempest. Then a fierce cry of rage would burst out like a thunderclap piercing the clouds."

"This state was too violent to last. . . . Yet the insurrection had no appearance of order; it was a blind movement; no one commanded, no one obeyed."

It was then that Camille Desmoulins, who had been conferring with the Orléanists, leapt on to a table brandishing a pistol, and called the people to arms. Issuing forth from the gardens, the wild mob surged through the streets, shouting and raving. Then a curious thing happened. In passing the waxwork exhibition of M. Curtius in the Boulevard du Temple, the busts of Necker and the Duke of Orléans were seized and paraded in triumph. They seemed to "spring from the ground," according to Desmoullins. This carefully planned gesture gave the mob a rallying point. In the Place Louis XV. the mob was met by troops under the command of the Prince de Lambese. The wax bust of the Duke of Orléans fell into the gutter during the disorder that followed and a man in a green coat—a linen draper's clerk, named Pepin— was slightly wounded in the leg when trying to rescue it. This was a godsend to the agitators. Pepin was rushed to the Palais Royal, where he displayed his wounded leg, crying, "To arms, citizens! The Dragoons have fired on the people and I myself have received a wound."

"This," wrote the Englishman, Dr. Rigby, who was in the crowd, "acted like an electric shock."

.   .   .   .   .   .

While this whirlpool of insurrection was gathering strength and the name of Orléans was echoing through the scorching day, Philippe had left Paris and gone on a fishing party to his chateau in the forest of Bondy, about nine miles out of Paris. With him were Prince Louis d'Aremburg and Mrs. Grace Dalrymple Elliot, the young and beautiful Scotchwoman who had been one of his mistresses in London and had remained a friend after he had left her for Agnès Buffon. The party dined early and returned to Paris that evening about eight o'clock. The night that followed was one of terror. "The streets were full of mob and soldiers, with symptoms of alarm—shouts—firing of arms— the ringing of large bells—the glare of torches and the appearance of distant fires." During the night Philippe remained in his house at Monceau, where Madame de Buffon joined him. Mrs. Elliot, to whom the news of the rioting was unexpected, went to find out what state public opinion was in and found many of the people in the streets "very violent in the Duke's favour, others as violent against him, these latter accusing him of wanting to dethrone the King." She does not say how Philippe received this information, but when she "tried to make him sensible of his errors" he only laughed at her, saying that "she was a proud Scotchwoman who loved nothing but kings and princes." When she persisted and entreated him to go to the King and offer his services "he was very angry with me and asked me whether I was paid by his enemies to give him such advice. . . . I went home extremely unhappy, for I saw that he was at open war with the King."

A most illuminating comment shows how thoroughly the Duke's partisans were preparing his advent to power. "The mob," wrote Mrs. Elliot, "obliged every one to wear a green cockade for two days, but afterwards they took red, white and blue, the Orléans livery."

Mrs. Elliot is inaccurate again, although her intention is clear. The cockade was at first red and blue: these were not only the colours of the city of Paris, but by a singular accident those of the livery of Orléans. "Lafayette, struck by the circumstance, and wishing to nationalize the ancient French colour by uniting it with the colours of the Revolution, proposed to the Hôtel de Ville the tri-coloured cockade." But it was after the King had accepted the new colours, blue and red, that Lafayette was struck by the circumstance and added the white. One wonders what Laclos thought as he watched the ceremony.

The following day, the 13th, it was resolved that a certain number of the more respectable inhabitants should be enrolled and immediately take arms. . . . This important and most necessary resolution was executed with wonderful promptitude and unexampled good management. . . . The citizen militia, it must be repeated, was armed in order to control the rabble. "This disarming the populace and establishing a well-armed military body of citizens may be considered as one of the most important steps which could have been taken by the Parisians at this period of the Revolution, and the extraordinary address and temper they discovered in doing it will probably ever be nurtured with admiration. By the morning of the 14th some sort of order had been restored. In the streets were no longer seen a rude and threatening populace; it had given place to the citizen soldiers, not only to defend the city, but even to undertake an enterprise of no trifling magnitude."

The formation of the militia was a severe check to

the Orléanist agitators. During the night of the 13th plans were drawn up for an attack on the Bastille, and the most furious of the Orléanist leaders, Jean Jacques Danton,[1] made his first appearance in the Revolution by thundering the prodigious lie that an army of 30,000 men was preparing to march on Paris and massacre the inhabitants.

"It is certain that the taking of the Bastille was planned, and that the day before plans of attack had been drawn up," wrote the authors of one of the earliest histories of the Revolution.

This was a shrewd move. By turning the panic against the brigands into a panic against the troops the leaders would have an even greater force behind them besides making the insurrection appear a rising of the people against the Court. This, in fact, is what happened. The militia had largely disarmed the brigands. More arms must be obtained, and the rumour was spread that the Court Party had stored huge supplies of rifles and ammunition in the Bastille. Other rumours spread like wildfire. "The people," cried the orators, "are being massacred. We must have arms for protection and vengeance."

Then to the incongruous cries of "Arms! Arms!" and "Vive le Roi!" the mob converged on the Bastille, and the event was snatched out of the hands of the Orléanist leaders to assume an heroic significance that no amount of analysis has ever altered. Every moment of that immortal day has been told and

---

[1] Danton was a paid and perfidious agent of the Duke of Orléans and rejected for his venality by 42 out of 48 sections of Paris (Aulard). Danton was all his life an Orléanist (Madelin).

retold in minutest detail, with its wild mixtures of heroism and brutality, of crime and glory, and does not need retelling here.

.   .   .   .   .   .

Mrs. Elliot declares that Philippe remained at Monceau and that Lafayette and Bailly came to consult him about the events which were going on in Paris. The second part of the statement is manifestly untrue, as Lafayette was Vice-President of the Assembly, and had been up all night in the permanent session. He did not learn until the evening of the taking of the Bastille, and not until the following day, the 15th, did he go to Paris, when he was acclaimed commander of the militia and became practical dictator of Paris, an unforeseen turn in events which completely upset the results that the Orléanists anticipated. It is interesting to compare this spontaneous demonstration with the organised demonstration in favour of the Duke of Orléans three days earlier. In both cases the exhibition of a bust was the signal; but the shouting around the wax bust of Philippe had been kept up by a few frenzied followers—the acclamation that followed the gesture of the president of the electors, Moreau de St. Mercy, was triumphant and unanimous. The Orléanists did not forget it. That same bust some time previous to the 10th August, 1792, became the source of daily quarrels between the Jacobins, who wished to have it removed from the Hôtel de Ville, and the national guard, who wished it to remain.

"These quarrels were on the point of becoming sanguinary. On the 10th August the bust was reduced to atoms and a medal voted by the town bearing the effigy of Lafayette was broken by the public executioner on the demand and in the presence of Danton."

The technique of revolution appears to be even less alterable than the stuff from which busts are made.

But if Philippe's wax bust is the only distinguishable thing about him on July 14th, there are other figures closely related to him whose appearance is both spectacular and significant. Madame le Brun, walking on the 13th of July with a friend near the Invalides, was about to turn back to her house in fear of the crowd of hideous creatures who haunted the Palais Royal, when she saw in the distance a young woman on horseback, in a riding habit and hat with long black feathers. Immediately the crowd parted and made way for her. She was followed by two grooms in the Orléans livery. "I at once recognised the lovely Pamela, who had been introduced to me by Mme de Genlis. She was in the zenith of her beauty, and was really exquisite. We heard the band of ruffians shout, ' Voilà, voilà! There is the one we must have for our queen!' Pamela kept pacing to and fro amongst this disgusting crowd, which saddened me very much."

On the morning of the 14th, when Mme de Genlis was told of the events in the city, she hurried with her pupils, the Duc de Chartres and the Duc de Montpensier, to the new terraces recently built by Beaumarchais, a friend of Philippe's, where they had a splendid view of the attack on the Bastille "without concealing their delight and enthusiasm." That night, with Pamela and the young Duc de Chartres, future King of the French, she went to the gardens of the Palais Royal and witnessed the indescribable orgy of exaltation, hysteria, obscenity and drunkenness which greeted the downfall of that symbol of despotism.

It needed but a gesture from a patriotic prince to turn all this into a triumph for himself and his party. Philippe made a gesture the following day—but it was neither patriotic nor triumphant.

CHAPTER XXI

O N the morning of the 15th Philippe presented himself at the doors of the Royal Council Chamber and demanded of the Baron de Breteuil, who was coming out, if he could speak to His Majesty. The minister pointed out that the King did not want to see any one, but that his highness could write to him if he had something to ask him, or that if he preferred to address the letter to him (Breteuil) he would communicate its contents that evening to His Majesty.

The Duke preferred the latter course, but instead of demanding the position of Lieutenant-General of the Realm, as he should have done according to the instructions of the plotters of Montrouge, he was content to beg M. de Breteuil to ask the King on his behalf for permission to go to England, which he proposed doing if events took a worse turn.

He could have been King on that day had he wanted to. Instead, he asked permission to go to England from the King he was supposed to dethrone—and not even directly, but by means of the minister who had served the *lettre de cachet* on him and whom he had told a short while before in a contemptuous tone to get up behind his coach in the flunkey's place.

What conclusions are to be drawn from this first ridiculous failure of the dreaded conspiracy?

"It is difficult to believe," wrote Beaulieu sarcastically, "that the Duke of Orléans, who had plenty of spirit, would have accepted the advice to demand of a king of France to kindly step down off his throne and give it to him. The Duke's counsellors knew well enough that if the plan were to succeed it would have to be by violent means—and these means were already in action. Why they failed is because the chief persons who wanted a change were very far from having the same aims. They all wanted a revolution, but not a revolution with the same results.

"If it is true that the conspirators intended to execute their plot on the morning of July 15th, then one must agree that the authors of this great conspiracy were very far from being as able as they were supposed to be."

Philippe hovers behind that *if* in a disconcerting obscurity. For a moment he appears. When the official deputation from the Assembly to Paris was being made up Bailly asked him why he did not go with it. "It is not advisable for me to go—people would see no one but me." He drew back before an open trial of strength. The Revolution moved on, but there is nothing to show that the Orléanists were in the least put out by the action of their chief. In fact, all the evidence points to an increased activity. After July 14th, what Lafayette calls "the three intrigues" become more clearly defined: "the Court, the Orléanists, and the one that afterwards assumed the name of Jacobin. The two latter more frequently acted together than in concert. The Jacobins wished to make them-

selves feared; the Orléanists to conceal themselves."

Out of that concealment came acts of violence,
sudden riots and assassinations. "The populace is
guided by an invisible hand," wrote Lafayette two
days after he had tried in vain to prevent the murder
of the seventy-four-year-old minister Foulon and his
son-in-law, Berthier. To understand these murders, it
is only necessary to know that Foulon, like Lamoignon,
had advised the King to arrest the Duke of Orléans
and his followers in the Assembly, and under no
circumstances to allow the army to be separated from
his person, to identify himself with the Revolution by
examining the *cahiers* himself, and by granting the
wishes of the people to checkmate the schemes of the
factions. Louis XVI was far from being able to assume
such leadership, and Foulon was paid for his wise
advice with a wisp of hay.[1] "Foulon's death," wrote
Mirabeau, "cost hundreds of thousands of francs"
—400,000 livres, according to the Marquis de
Bouzolp, who declared that he knew that Laclos
had received that sum on the evening of July
16th to organise the riot which ended in the two
murders.

According to Mme Campan, Foulon's advice in the
form of two memoirs was read aloud by Mme Adelaide
in the presence of four or five people. One of them,
Comte Louis de Narbonne, was intimate with Mme
de Stael, Necker's daughter, and it was this liaison

[1] It is well known that the murderers spread the report that Foulon had
made the remark: "If the people lack bread, let them eat hay." A wisp of hay was
stuck between his dead lips. His head was cut off and carried about on a pike.

that gave the Queen reason to think that the opposition party knew of Foulon's memorandum.

All through Lafayette's memoirs from the fall of the Bastille to the October riots of the 5th and 6th the conspiracy keeps appearing, now obscurely referred to in the most general terms, now in violent tones of perplexity, and now in some revealing picture. "Our subsistences go very badly. All hell conspires against us," he wrote three days after Foulon's murder.

One day, riding near the district of the Cordeliers Club, the stronghold of the extreme left, he was asked to come in. The assembly was numerous. The hall was partly filled by French guards. After the usual acclamations "the well-known Danton," president and orator of the day, informed Lafayette that to recompense the patriotism of the brave French guards, the district had decided to demand that the regiment should be established in their former state and that their command should be given to the first prince of the blood, the Duke of Orléans."

"No doubt is entertained," said Danton, "of the consent of the general-in-chief to such a patriotic proposal." Danton added some compliments and the club applauded.

Lafayette remarked that he was able to dissuade the citizens and the guards themselves from such a project. "The conspiracy of which the roots were in a different quarter was completely overthrown."

Certainly the regiment of the French guard under Orléanist command and surrounded with patriotic memories would have been a deadly and possibly

decisive weapon ·in any future tumult. Lafayette's
only mistake—and it was a big one—was in that word
completely. His love of the Revolution combined with
his vanity to make him despise the plots that surrounded him.

Yet during August and September rumours became
alarming. Everything pointed to an organised and
serious disturbance. The shortage of grain continued
in spite of the creation of a committee specially
appointed to deal with it. "If bread should not fail,
I can answer for all things," exclaimed Lafayette.
But bread did fail with mysterious regularity. Not
only was the committee singularly inadequate, but it
is known that large shipments were sent abroad.
Gouverneur Morris, whose observant eye saw most
of what was going on, offered grain from America
as part payment of the American debt, the settlement
of which he was charged with negotiating. It would
have been a godsend to the city. There were
objections. The time needed to transport it was too
great. There were mysterious delays in negotia-
tion. The suggestion was side-tracked. And, though
there were plenty of people who viewed with horror
the acts of violence that were constantly taking
place and who were ready to oppose them with all
their influence and power, yet when you have hunger
on the side of anarchy your best intentions to combat
it must fail. "It is easier for me to place 80,000 men
under arms," wrote Lafayette, "than to make the
arrangements the committee of supply has full right
to require. To this labour I shall most assiduously

MADAME DE GENLIS

devote myself, and I am sensible of its vast importance."

Enough is known of the grain speculation of '89[1] to reveal a refinement of corruption and a callousness towards human beings difficult to believe. In spite of a very mixed amount of evidence men are inclined to believe in some way or another in a certain natural goodness in human nature; and to come upon carefully planned wrecking and calculated cruelty is something of a shock, more especially at a time when excessive confidence in the perfectibility of the human race was accepted as a cardinal point of faith.

Since July, 1788, the circulation of grain had had to be under the protection of troops. When it was not guarded some such event as the following would occur:

Wagon-loads of wheat would be conducted mysteriously out of Paris. The drivers would be ordered to say that they were loads of salt and rice for Havre. Suddenly a young girl or an old peasant woman would slash open one of the sacks with a knife or a scythe and wheat would pour out on the ground. A riot would burst out and the rumour would spread that it was the aristocrats who were taking the wheat away from Paris, that they wanted to starve the people, etc. etc. Meanwhile the drivers and their carts would disappear during the rioting.

During the summer months Philippe himself kept very much in the background. His name was on

---

[1] For account and dates of grain speculations during 1789, see G. Bord, *Conspiration de '89.*

everybody's lips, a legend of evil to the royalists, a
symbol of hope to the rabble, a subject of speculation
to the constitutional liberals. These last, among whom
were Mounier, Lafayette and Bailly, found themselves
already in the position of firemen trying to put out
the blaze which they themselves had helped to light,
a position that every group in turn was destined to
take up until the flames themselves had consumed the
whole house, all the fire brigade, and died from sheer
weariness of burning.

Meanwhile "the organisation of disorder" continued rapidly.

Montmorin, the Foreign Minister, was at his wits'
end, and his wits were not very long. During the last
days of September the designs of the Orléanists were
causing him acute anxiety. There was only one
source of armed power in Paris—Lafayette's National
Guard. Towards the end of September Montmorin
spoke to him of becoming not only Constable, but
even Lieutenant-General of the Kingdom. Lafayette's
reply was characteristic. He said that such a situation
would neither increase his credit in France nor
strengthen his determination to defend the King
against the Duke of Orléans. He told Montmorin that
he advised the King in case of any unforeseen conspiracy to come at once to Paris, where the National
Guard would protect him. Yet so far from adequate
did this advice seem to Montmorin that he sent
Mounier to Paris on purpose to add his great personal
influence in trying to persuade the general to change
his mind. Again Lafayette refused.

While these subterranean events were going on the conspiracy reared its head in the National Assembly, and though it was supported by Mirabeau, it was defeated. During the stormy debates on the royal veto, "the Duke of Orléans was among the ardent men, or at least those who appeared to be ardent, who rejected every sort of royal sanction." On September 16th the question of the succession to the throne was introduced by the Baron de Juigné. It seemed on the face of it an acceptable decree. It declared the inviolability of the King, the heredity and indivisibility of the throne, and was received with approval by the majority. The decree ended by stating that the Crown was hereditary in the ruling branch from male to male by order of the primogeniture to the perpetual exclusion of women and of their descendants.

Under this apparently conventional decree was hidden dynamite.

"I observe," said the distinguished lawyer Target, "that before decreeing the order of succession to the throne, the Assembly ought to decide if the ruling house of Spain (directly descended from Louis XIV.) would be able to reign in France, although it has renounced its right to the claim by authentic treaties."

The Orléanists immediately demanded an adjournment. The recognition of the rights of the Spanish Bourbons would exclude the House of Orléans. Mirabeau declared that there was no case for deliberation at the moment. Sillery supported him and Target withdrew his motion. But the following day the violent discussion still continued. Mirabeau tried to

cover up the Orléanist retreat by an adroit move. He
raised the question of the regency, and gave it a
patriotic turn by moving that no one can exercise the
function of regency unless he has been born in France.
At the moment when this motion was introduced the
eyes of the whole Assembly turned to where the Duke
of Orléans was accustomed to sit. His place was
empty. Philippe, who had known how his party
intended to manœuvre, had left the hall a moment
before. Immediately after Mirabeau's motion, Sillery
intervened by drawing from his pocket a copy of the
letters patent of 1713, connected with the Treaty of
Utrecht, which contained an act of renunciation to
the French throne by Philip V.

The tumult following this reading was immense.
It was apparent that the question had resolved itself
into one of recognition of the rights of the Orléans
branch of the Bourbons to be next in line as legitimate
heirs to the throne or to the regency.

D'Espremeuil spread consternation among the
Orléanists by bringing the whole question out into the
light. "I am not speaking," he said, "either for the
Spanish branch or the Orléans branch. I am speaking
for the French maxim. This maxim in the order of
succession to the throne is the salic law consecrated by
our fathers, by the Estates General, and by our constituents. The throne is hereditary in the reigning
branch from male to male by order of primogeniture.
The renunciation of the King of Spain is an exception
to this rule. The exception must not prevent the
establishment of the principle. And in any case," he

added, "if the question is ever raised it will not be decided by decrees but by canon."

Mirabeau, Duport and others attempted to strike out the question of succession and declare simply the inviolability of the throne. It was said, according to Ferrière, a deputy of the nobles, that, seeing the impossibility of obtaining this amendment, Mirabeau threatened to use more violent means, and that the president, Clermont Tonnerre, adjourned the session.

During that evening the only subject discussed was the question of succession to the throne. A friend of Mirabeau remarked that the dangerous question of Spanish succession would probably never arrive, as there were so many members of the present French royal family.

"As a matter of fact," said Mirabeau, "the question is not so remote as you think. The apathetic state of the King and Monsieur can well shorten their days and make the whole question depend on the existence of the dauphin."

"I'm surprised," said his friend, "that you have forgotten the existence of M. le Comte d'Artois and his children."

"If the occasion should ever arise, one could consider the Comte d'Artois (who had emigrated), as well as his children as fugitives and extra lex."

The following day the Assembly was again the scene of violent debate. Finally the decree that passed contained the phrase: "Sans entendre rien préjudicier sur l'effet des renonciations"—which left the question of succession exactly where it had been before. One point, however, it made clearer. A majority of the Assembly was ready to resist the Orléanists legally in their pretensions to the throne. This made revolutionary methods essential to any chance of success.

The end of the debate had something comic about it. Philippe had purposely stayed away from the hall during the two days' wrangling. It gave his friend a free hand. But now Sillery leapt to his feet and cried angrily, "I demand that it be written in the minutes that this decree was passed in the absence of the Duke of Orléans."

"I demand," interrupted a royalist deputy, le Marquis de Mirepoix, with elaborate irony, "that it be added that it was passed in the absence of the King of Spain."

This was the political prelude to what Lafayette declared was the most violent and the most general tumult he had ever witnessed.

CHAPTER XXII

THE OCTOBER DAYS

THE march on Versailles was the Orléanists' supreme bid for power. Every possible means of propaganda had been used, every possible method of instigation and intimidation had been resorted to during the weeks between the fall of the Bastille and the morning of October 5th. The mob orators of the Palais Royal, such as St. Hurougue, had been going full blast. A murky little mortal named Marat, formerly "physician to the stables of the Comte d'Artois," had reappeared in Paris and had begun his shouting journalism. Anonymous letters had been sent to the moderate members of the Assembly, threatening death and pillage. One of them to Clermont Tonnerre began with this edifying phrase: "The patriotic assembly of the Palais Royal has the honour to inform you, etc. . . . that if the ignorant and corrupt members (to be found, naturally from the clergy and the aristocrats) continue their tactics, 15,000 men are ready to burn their chateaux and their houses, and yours in particular, Monsieur."

Agents of the Palais Royal were everywhere in evidence. It was known that pikes were being manufactured in large quantities. Not only pikes, but medals with the head of the Duke of Orléans were struck in

readiness. Under the figurehead was inscribed:
"Father of his Country."

Two further attempts were made to gain Lafayette's
support. One of them on September 21st and the
second during the morning of October 5th. On
September 21st Lafayette was informed that there was
a plot at Versailles to seize the Duke of Orléans, disperse the Assembly, carry off the King and cut the
throats of M. Lafayette and M. Bailly. This clumsy
attempt to link the names of Orléans and Lafayette
had no more success than the more direct approaches
had had. Still Laclos did not despair of winning over
the General. Already he had his outposts in the
National Guard. One of them, Santerre, a brewer in
the Faubourg St. Antoine, was destined to play a
notorious part in the Revolution.

On the morning of October 5th, Lafayette not only
heard the words "council of regency" among the
enormous sea of voices, but he was actually offered
the regency by a young man named Mercier, at about
eleven o'clock in the morning. He had been summoned to the Hôtel de Ville by news of the mob rising
and was in the hall of the committee of police, presided
over by the Abbé Fauchet. Fauchet was a violent
Orléanist at the time. As though it had been planned,
the young grenadier Mercier, followed by a great
number of his fellow-grenadiers, formerly French
guards, and an immense crowd of people, burst into
the room where Mercier repeated his lesson well.
"My General," he cried, "the King deceives us all, and
you as well as others. We must depose him. His child

shall be our King, you shall be regent, and all things will go well." This last attempt failed like the rest. But it made clear that the march on Versailles was not a spontaneous movement of famished people clamouring for bread, but was planned for the express purpose of deposing the King.

Every hour of October 5th to 6th has been examined again and again in monumental detail. The more light that is thrown upon the whole affair the more does it appear one of the most disgraceful, farcical, tragic, bloodthirsty scenes in history. One asks: Were there no men in France, or at least in Paris? Was it all a mist of melodrama, a boiling cauldron of brains with a pinch of famine thrown in? Was there nobody to stand against the ridiculous, fantastic and terrible crowd of half-organised hoodlums and riff-raff marching in the rags of revolutionary bunkum—in reality out for loot, wine and murder? Where were the nobility—where were the counts, marquises and dukes who thought their toes were being trod on by the new order of things? Where were the *Tiers d'État*, representatives of twenty-five millions? There were plenty of them, apparently, who were willing to witness the scene and throw their blame on any one else—chiefly on the Duke of Orléans. What were they doing on the grand staircase the following morning during the rush of the mob? What were they doing in the courtyards, at the windows? Like every one else in the Revolution, they were looking on; like every one else, they supposed they were either victims or instruments of the blind force called revolution—

they forgot that they were men. It only needed a man with a little spirit and ordinary courage to control the situation. It only needed a handful of National Guards drawn up in battle order to sweep the riff-raff out of the palace without even resorting to gunfire—though ready, and meaning to do so if necessary.

Lafayette was not a great general, and he was honest enough to know it; but he was a man, at least when he did not take valuable time to stop, take out his conscience and consult his principles. And on this occasion he and his few guards were the only men present. All the great word-spinners in the Assembly, all the constitution makers, lawyers, priests and politicians could not even control a mob from the slums of the capital—not a leader among them. Mirabeau himself was committed to the murder plot until he saw the work of the conspiracy collapse. Then he was adroit enough to change his colour under cover of a smoke-screen of oratory.

Where was Philippe during the October days? Did he take part in the riot? His name was continually on the lips of the wildest of the mob. "Long live our King Orléans—our Father Orléans," re-echoes again and again from those savage voices.

All the evidence shows that he was at Versailles in the Chateaux and the courtyards during the fatal morning of the 6th. The only question that remains is, whether or not he was there between five and six in the morning or whether, as he himself stated,[1] he

---

[1] *L'Exposé de la conduite de M. le Duc d'Orléans redigé par lui même à Londres* (June, 1790).

arrived between nine and eleven. The difference of
those four hours is vital. At about five-fifteen the
Paris mob, which had quietened down during the
night, was marshalled in the Place d'Armes with
drums and banners. They were promptly divided into
several columns as if individuals recognised several
leaders (Mounier's report from Geneva). Until then
there had been no bloodshed, though there had been
indiscriminate shooting. Beaulieu wrote that he had
gone to bed with the uncomfortable sound of whistling
bullets in his ears. Nothing more serious had occurred
than the disgraceful scenes of the night before when
the Assembly had been invaded by bedraggled and
drunken men disguised as women who shouted for
bread and Mirabeau. From 5.15 in the morning of
the 6th the farce turned into a tragedy. It is strange
that the mob should have found a way into the palace
unless it were led by some one who knew exactly
where to get in. It is strange, but it is not proof that
Philippe was that some one.

The story of the next hour and a half has been
written and rewritten. The murder and beheading of
the two bodyguards—the flight of Marie Antoinette
—Lafayette's arrival with the National Guard. By
nine o'clock order had been restored in the palace.
The King had promised to go with his family to Paris,
and the Orléanist plot had failed.

Where was Philippe during that hour and a half
when the mob was making desperate attempts to murder the Queen? In the inquiry instituted by the Court
of the Châtelet, which lasted for the next eight months,

388 witnesses were questioned and submitted signed
and sworn statements of what they had seen, what
they had heard, and what they had heard said during
the two days. Besides this immense jumble of evidence
there are statements by Mounier and other deputies,
who resigned their seats in the National Assembly and
retired in disgust and in protest after October 6th.
There is a statement by Philippe, written in London
the following June, which claims to be a record of the
movements during the two days, and there is an
account written by Grace Elliott eleven years later,
which attempts to establish an alibi that unfortunately
is quite different from that which Philippe claimed for
himself. Her attempt is pathetically inaccurate. "I
must here do justice to the Duke of Orléans," she
wrote. "He certainly was not at Versailles on that
dreadful morning, for he breakfasted with company
at my house when he was accused of being in the
Queen's apartments disguised. He told us then that he
heard the fishwomen had gone to Versailles with some
of the Faubourgs, and that people said they were gone
to bring the King again to Paris. . . . He added that
it must be a scheme of Lafayette's. ' I dare say that
they will accuse me of it, as they lay every tumult at
my door.' He stayed at my house until half-past one
o'clock. I have no reason to suppose that he went to
Versailles till late in the afternoon, when he went to
the States, as every one knows."

Nothing in this account agrees with Philippe's
own alibi. According to him he slept at the Palais
Royal on the night of the 5th, and the following

morning towards eight o'clock he started for the
National Assembly. Mrs. Elliott's attempt to put the
blame on Lafayette gives the show away. Nobody
except the Orléanists had any idea of putting any
blame on Lafayette. Moreover, no written evidence
accused Philippe of being in the palace disguised.
One of the few points of agreement among the
crowd of witnesses is the colour of his coat on that
morning—a top coat, grey in colour.

Among the huge mass of remaining evidence only
one witness testified to having seen Philippe among
the murderous mob on the staircase: M. de la Serre,
chevalier of the royal and military order of Saint-
Louis, brigadier in the armies of the King, living in
Paris, rue Favart 4, witness No. 226. This gentleman
declared that he had been in the King's apartments
on October 5th, and that he had encountered and
spoken to the deputation of women who had been
granted an audience with His Majesty, that one of
the women had exclaimed that the King was a good
king and a father to them all; that another woman
had interrupted and said, "The Duke of Orléans is
our father," and that he, the witness, had objected
to this. That he had gone home about two in the
morning after M. de Lafayette had assured him and
others that everything was tranquil. At six o'clock on
the morning of the 6th he returned to the chateau by
the *place des armes* where he saw a great movement
of the people; that he then ran to the cour royale,
then he joined the people and ascended the great
marble staircase; that these people were uttering

imprecations, saying, "Our father is with us, let us march!" That he asked one of these men who their father was. This man answered him, "Sacre Dieu, don't you know him—the Duke of Orléans." That he asked the man, "Where is he? Is he here?" The witness had then reached the first flight of the staircase. This man answered him by indicating with a gesture of his arm that the Duke was at the top of the staircase. "Eh, damnation, don't you see him? He is there! He is there!" Then the witness, raising his head and standing on tiptoe, saw the Duke of Orléans at the head of the people making a gesture with his arm to indicate the hall of the Queen's bodyguard, and that the Duke of Orléans then turned to the left to reach the King's apartments.

During the morning he was seen by six other witnesses, and although none of their evidence could be considered seriously in a court of law, some of it gives a glimpse of Philippe on that tragic morning. The Vicomte de la Châtre, aged 57, deputy at the National Assembly, an extreme royalist, witness number 127, declared that on the morning of the 6th October he heard piercing cries of "Vive le roi d'Orléans!" and that he looked out of his window towards the courtyard of the Ministers, where he saw the Duke of Orléans "at this moment walking along the line of troops a little way in front of them, looking as though he had come from the *place des armes* where the bodyguards, two in number, had been killed that same morning. This prince had a switch in his hand and a big cockade in his hat, and never stopped laughing. I saw him disappear, followed by a big crowd of people, and he never stopped laughing and playing with his switch."

This sounds authentic enough, but as no time is indicated by the phrase "at this moment," it can merely be taken as evidence that Philippe walked across the courtyard of the Ministers some time during the morning, smiling or laughing and playing with a light cane while a part of the rabble cheered him.

Another deputy, César de Guilherung, 29 years old, procurator of the King, an extreme royalist, knows that M. de Lartigues, bodyguard of the King, said that he saw the Duke of Orléans walking among the brigands, who broke into the chateau, October 6th, about six in the morning.

Interesting, but useless as evidence. M. de Lartigues never appeared to verify this second-hand statement. Besides, de la Serre and others were also walking about among the brigands that morning, according to their own statements.

Another witness was the maidservant of Mme la Tour du Pin, who had an apartment in the palace. The maid, whose name was Marguerite, rushed into her mistress's room early in the morning. She said that she had been in the courtyard, where the body-guards had just been massacred, and that a monsieur arrived on the scene with very muddy boots and a whip in his hand, who was no other than the Duke of Orléans, whom she knew quite well from having often seen him; that also the wretches surrounding him

showed their joy, crying out, "Vive notre roi d'Orléans!" while he signed them to be silent.

About the same time he was seen in the Cour de
Marbre walking with Duport, whom he held under
the arm and with whom he was talking in a very gay
and easy manner. (Marquis de Digoine, 168th witness.)

Later in the day, when the huge procession accompanying the King to Paris made its slow way through
Passy, Philippe was observed standing on the terrace
of the Maison Boulain-villiers with his children and
Mme de Genlis beside him. There was sporadic
cheering from some of the crowd, which appeared to
embarrass him. He made signs to them to stop and
tried to hide himself behind his children. But the
cheering only redoubled and "pointed him out as *le
roi du jour*." Whereupon he withdrew before the
royal coach passed. But Mme de Genlis was not in
the least embarrassed as she watched the humiliation
of the royal family led captive by the raging mob that
had invaded the palace a few hours before. She appeared to enjoy the scene very much, and Philippe's
daughter, Mlle d'Orléans, was convulsed with laughter
at the sight of the Queen's plight. Long afterwards
Mme de Genlis denied that she was even there at all,
but here, as elsewhere, she was exercising her unusual
gift of forgetting what was embarrassing to remember.

Lafayette, riding beside the royal coach, saw that
group on the terrace and turned to the Comte d'Estaing
with disgust, saying that what he had witnessed at
the palace that morning had made a royalist of him.

The following day Philippe was to feel the result of that disgust.

The book that contains the report of the Châtelet is "like a café where one hears a thousand confused and contradictory assertions." Out of its pages comes the picture of Philippe in a grey top coat, round hat, a switch in his hand, smiling and talking gaily, cheered by a crowd of brigands. Nothing more than that, unless we are to take the solitary assertion of la Serre, that he waved his arm towards the Queen's apartments and then disappeared in the other direction. Even such a vague act of leadership is so contrary to his character that it is difficult to believe. Would it not have been heard of by others who were only too eager to implicate him? In fact "the judges of the Châtelet give the impression of making a personal affair of what should be an impartial matter of law." This remark was made by a contemporary critic of the whole affair who condemns the lack of order and clumsiness of the report in a remarkable sentence. "It should have examined," says this commentator, "whether or not the insurrection was connected with the famine in Paris, whether the scarcity of bread was connected with the 12th July (beginning of the Bastille riots), whether the 12th July had any connection with the 28th of April (the Reveillon Riot), whether these three fatal days had anything to do with the burning of thirty-six chateaux, with the brigands that overran the provinces, whether all the rebel movements among the troops and in the towns can be traced to the same impulse: in a word, if the same fatal project was attacking France on every side."

This is the true approach, and the more closely the evidence is examined the more clearly Philippe emerges, not as the leader but as the led, not as the instigating but as the consenting power. There is a tragedy of futility in that group on the terrace in Passy. His enemies were eager to make him a leader of murderers. It seems more probable that at that moment he was a prince of cads.

CHAPTER XXIII

EXILED

LAFAYETTE'S evidence concerning the October days is necessarily among the most important. He wrote that the dangers dreaded from the Orléanist party had passed away after October 6th; "but the spirit of the faction was not destroyed, and its chief possessed means of intrigue from his fortune, connections and immorality of conduct which it was important to oppose." There was but one method of proving his weakness—to attack him in person.

On October 7th Philippe received a note from the General, requesting a meeting that afternoon at the house of the Marquise de Coigny. The meeting was very imperious on one side and very resigned on the other. "It was settled," wrote Lafayette, "that the Duke should set out for London with a sort of mission to account for his departure. . . ."

"The King has descended several steps of his throne," said Lafayette, "but I have placed myself on the last; he will descend no further; and in order to reach him you will have to pass over my body. You have cause for complaint against the Queen, and so have I, but the time has come to forget all grievances."

It was a strange interview. Both men were exquisitely polite. Mrs. Elliot wrote afterwards that

" they met as friends. They were on the best of terms."
Lafayette had already conceived a plan of action. He
suggested that the Duke's many connections with
England could be most valuable at the moment. He
had so many friends and so many interests there. He
was, in fact, the person most suitable for a diplomatic
mission. It was necessary to discover the intentions
of the English Court towards the Low Countries
which were in revolt against the Emperor Joseph II.
The Duke was known to be interested in revolutions.
It was possible when the time came to put a prince
at the head of the revolt that the Duke might be in
the most favourable position, especially if he knew
the viewpoint of the English Court.

Philippe listened. His thirst for vengeance on the
Queen had been more than satisfied. This new idea
seemed to offer an escape from a world that was becoming more involved than he had expected. Lafayette
continued talking. The Duke's name covered a
number of dangerous intrigues. It would be to his
own advantage, as well as to the advantage of the
country, if he were to undertake the mission. Philippe
was persuaded.

That same night Mirabeau and Biron changed his
mind for him—a note was sent to Lafayette, who
immediately replied that if it would be convenient
for him to-morrow after dinner to pay another visit
to Madame de Coigny, "I shall take advantage of the
occasion to say a few words that may interest him."

Lafayette's words interested Philippe to such an
extent that once again he promised to leave—this time

within twenty-four hours. Lafayette thereupon took Philippe to the King, "who was much astonished, especially when the Duke of Orléans, having assured him that he would endeavour to discover at London the authors of these troubles," Lafayette interrupted, saying, "You are more interested in that than any one else, for no one is as badly compromised as you are."

Once again Mirabeau interfered. He called Biron, Philippe's great friend, and said to him, "Monsieur the Duke of Orléans, without any preliminary judgment, is going to quit the post that his constituents have confided to him. If he obeys Lafayette I shall denounce his departure and I shall oppose it. If he reveals the invisible hand that is sending him away I will denounce the authority which can take the place of the law—let him choose between these alternatives." Mirabeau knew all the tricks of the demagogue even to the point of invoking the law to defend some one who was implicated in a plot that savoured of murder and treason.

Philippe was sufficiently influenced by Mirabeau's support to write to Lafayette, saying that he had changed his mind again. He was like a shuttlecock between the General and Mirabeau. "The poor prince is decoyed," wrote Mirabeau to La Marck that evening, "or appears to be so by the hope of concluding the quadruple alliance. He is entrusted with a letter to the King of England. There is not a single proof against him, and if these should be invented there aren't any in reality. This becomes impudent. I've already told you, my dear count, that I will never bow my head except to the despotism of genius. Until to-morrow in the Assembly. *Vale et me ama.*"

But it was Lafayette's turn to strike. He immediately arranged a meeting at the Ministry of Foreign Affairs in the presence of the minister, Montmorin.

Philippe had recovered some composure. He knew that Mirabeau intended to denounce the idea of departure the next morning.

"My enemies pretend," he said to Lafayette, "that you have proofs against me."

"They must be mine rather who make such an assertion," answered Lafayette. "If I were able to produce proofs against you I should already have had you arrested. I am searching for them everywhere."

Philippe left in great agitation. He demanded his passports, which were granted without question. He wrote a letter to the King accepting his mission in the most devoted terms imaginable, and at five o'clock the next morning he got into his coach with Laclos and started for Boulogne.

At the morning session of the Assembly, Mirabeau was handed a note from Biron telling him what had happened. He passed it to one of his friends sitting next to him. "Look at this!" he exclaimed. "Read it. He's as cowardly as a lackey. He's a blackguard; he isn't worth the trouble one takes for him." He also said a number of other things that are unprintable.

The Orléans party had lost their main support in the Assembly.

Later in the morning another coach, carrying Agnès Buffon, set out on the road to Boulogne and London. At the same time a note was handed to Mme de Genlis from Philippe, saying that he would be away for a month. But it was not until nine months had passed that he returned to France.

CHAPTER XXIV

THE LONDON MISSION

THE travellers arrived at Boulogne early in the morning of the 11th and went to the *Lion d'Or* to wait until the time of sailing. News of Philippe's arrival spread rapidly. Some said that Laclos was making a last attempt to gain popular support for his *protégé*. The rumour spread that Philippe was being exiled by the Court; that the pretended mission was no more that "an honest *lettre de cachet*" in disguise. A delegation of sailors presented themselves to the local authorities and declared that the people would not allow the departure, as they regarded His Highness as the father of the people and they were afraid to be deprived of a powerful protector. In order to make sure that the passports had been granted by the Assembly, two municipal officials accompanied one of Philippe's secretaries named Clarke to Paris, where they were verified immediately, both by the Commune and the Assembly. Any hope of a triumphant and popular return that Laclos or Mirabeau, or any other member of the "party" may have had, was nipped in the bud. In fact public opinion in Paris had risen in a tirade of hatred against Philippe. The day after the passports had been verified and were on their way back to Boulogne, Mirabeau delivered a flowery speech praising Lafayette's behaviour in the crisis, thus openly reshuffling the complicated political game of intrigue. Philippe's friends, such as Sillery and La Touche, who attempted to excuse him to the Assembly, could not get a hearing and those who declared his journey was a voluntary one were laughed at.

Gouverneur Morris listening to the gossip at his club, found Philippe's friends "chopfallen although they defend him, which is absurd, for they know not enough of the matter to make an able defence, or if they do, conceal that knowledge, which is the same thing." The following day Morris heard that "the friends of the Duke of Orléans will denounce him to the National Assembly, so as to oblige him to return, they expecting that his popularity in Paris will make him triumph over his enemies." But Morris was late with the news. The attempt had already failed, and two days later he heard that the Duchess had received a note from the Duc de Biron that the Duke of Orléans embarked yesterday at nine in the morning with a fair wind.

There is one other remark reported by Morris which is significant. Mme de Flahaut, to whom both he and Talleyrand were attentive, told him that Lafayette had remarked in speaking of the Duke of Orléans, " *Les lettres de créance sont des lettres de grâce.*" The Duc de Biron hearing of this, wrote to Lafayette and received an answer in which he tells him, " *Je n'ai pas pu me servir d'une telle expression puisqu'il n'y a aucune preuve contre le duc d'Orléans.* She says she has seen the letters." This only confirms Lafayette's accounts in his memoirs where he never directly accuses the Duke of Orléans and blames the Châtelet for its extreme party spirit.

Philippe arrived in London on the 21st, and established himself at No. 3 Chappel Street, Park Lane, which he had rented beforehand.

Two days after his arrival the *Gentleman's Magazine* contained the following paragraph: "This morning the Duke of Orléans, the French Ambassador and another Foreign Nobleman went to Windsor on a visit to the King and the Royal Family. On the Duke's return to town he gave a grand dinner to several of the nobility and gentlemen from France at his house in Park Lane. The reports of his errand to England are various: nothing, however, has yet transpired to justify even a conjecture. It is certainly no trivial business: nor merely from motives of his own."

George III. had received Philippe none too graciously. He did not approve of anything he had heard about the events in France and he took no pains to hide it. The audience had a touch of malice under its formality and the royal tempers were not in their serenest mood as Philippe had arrived half an hour late which irritated Queen Caroline exceedingly. The King immediately launched into an eloquent eulogy of the French Royal Family and the admirable courage which the King and Queen had shown in the late disturbances, in spite of the startling fact that they had been deserted by those very people whose rank and position should have drawn them closer to the throne. There was no mistaking His Majesty's meaning, and Philippe was made to understand that the Revolution was rapidly be-

coming unpopular in England, where ideas of equality
have never gained much credence outside the regions
of the abstract. The English were in fact gathering the
fog of righteous indignation around them to combat
those principles which Burke declared would seriously
endanger their laws and liberties—or, as Tom Paine
put it, their places and pensions.

The stories that the emigrés told as they crowded
into London only tended to increase the abhorrence
of what was happening in France, and as the name of
Orléans was invariably, even monotonously, linked
with every act of violence, Philippe found himself as
universally shunned as he had formerly been flattered.
He had deserted his class and betrayed his party, the two
unforgivable sins.

In the face of this national lifted eyebrow and stony
stare he preserved the most complete indifference. He
lived quietly in Chappel Street for the next nine months.
"He rarely sees the minister," wrote M. La Luzerne,
the French Ambassador, in January, "he does not
think any more of his mission. His mistress, Mme de
Buffon, the club where he spends most of his time,
console him for all the chagrin he has suffered on the
other side of the Channel."

Yet his diplomatic correspondence with Montmorin
shows some glimmerings of intelligence which disturbed the Foreign Minister and interested Lafayette.
The fictitious mission might even have reached the
point of turning into a real one and resulted in some
sort of commercial entreaty if it had not been for the
dignified aloofness of the Duke of Leeds in London

and the marked lack of enthusiasm in Montmorin's dispatches from Paris. Two years later Montmorin informed the American Minister, Gouveneur Morris, that Philippe had tried to get an authority to offer a treaty, which was of course not granted. It was unlikely that those very people who had taken considerable trouble to get him out of the country, would then allow him to turn his exile into a means of recapturing his lost popularity.

As the months passed and every attempt to approach the subject of a treaty was met with the most polite evasions and exasperating delays, it is not unnatural that Philippe turned to his own affairs and pleasures. The Prince of Wales and Mrs. Fitzherbert and their circle of friends together with a very few emigrés such as Calonne were the only people he saw. At least, such was the report of the French Ambassador who had surrounded the house in Chappel Street with the inevitable spies. The presence of Calonne who came in the evenings gave rise to great activities among the spies, and a number of dark plots were immediately rushed to the Embassy and thence to Paris. Actually Philippe was trying to salvage a part of his huge and unwieldy fortune by transferring cash to London. It is ironic to learn that large sums were lost because he took so much care to have them transferred by secret routes in order not to raise questions in France. "It is from this moment," declared Talleyrand, "that his immense fortune began to disappear. The free funds of the Duke of Orléans all passed to London by roundabout ways and by secret agents who, because of their obscurity, were able to be unfaithful and enjoy the fruits of their swindling. Such is the opinion of those who were at the head of affairs."

Another matter of importance occupied Philippe while he was in London. He had promised Louis XVI. that he would do what he could to relieve the famine in Paris by releasing large stores of grain which were held by his agents in the Channel Islands. It was one of Philippe's outstanding characteristics that when he had given his word he kept it. Even his most violent enemy, Montjoie, concedes him this virtue and admits that "he was not incapable of doing good and that nature had put a certain loyalty in his soul." And it is Montjoie himself who declares that Philippe kept this pledge to the King and released so much grain that within two months of his arrival in England hundreds of grain wagon convoys were leaving the coasts of Normandy for Paris and the provinces, and the famine had disappeared. The whole history of grain speculation is shrouded in rumour and the amount involved in Philippe's speculations is unknown, but the fact remains that his most assiduous detractor, who was in Paris at the time, gives him credit for an action that was both generous and disinterested. There were only too many who were ready to accuse him of having caused the famine. But it is more noteworthy to find one who grudgingly praises his "very astonishing conduct" in helping to relieve it during his sojourn in London.

Mme de Buffon told Mirabeau's friend, La Marck, long afterwards that Philippe proposed to her at this time to go to America and live there together. She refused, she said, giving as a pretext that she would not be able to survive the regrets which the Duke of Orléans might have for having done so rash a thing.

Instead of going to America he went to Newmarket, and then took his mistress on a tour of England, following the race meetings all over the country. There are glimpses of him at the trial of Warren Hastings, and Morris, then in London, met him at Mrs. Church's ball where, he wrote, "things are really magnificent and well-conducted. The royal brothers and Mrs. Fitzherbert are among the guests. The Duke of Orléans also is here, with whom I exchange a few words." Morris never neglected to nod to royalty and record it in his diaries.

Philippe's letters from London show how easy it would have been at this time to draw the poison out of his feud against the Queen and make him at the same time a supporter of the constitution. A little flattery, a little management by those in Paris who wasted their time being afraid of him, would have done the trick. His proposal to go to America with his mistress shows that he was sick of the Revolution. The feebleness of his ambition refused to accept the heroic part which men had imagined for him. Yet those who persisted in regarding him as the unique source of trouble were still too impressed by the glitter of titles and the glamour of inherited privileges to understand the emptiness behind them. In fact, hearing of the meetings with Calonne, Lafayette imagined a plot in which his two most detested opponents, the

aristocrats and the Orléanists, would unite in a counter
revolution aided by fabulous English gold. At the
moment when Philippe could have been dropped into a
harmless diplomatic niche he was confronted with one
of Lafayette's *aides-de-campe*, M. de Bonnville, who
informed him in a courteous rhetoric that if he returned to France the General would challenge him the
following day. This was giving Philippe too much
importance but it was still difficult to think in terms
of the new freedom, and men were struggling with
phantasies of their own creating quite as fiercely as
with reality.

On December 29th, Philippe sent letters with New
Year's greetings to the King and Queen written in the
most respectful terms. He begged them not to judge
him by rumours spread by his enemies and protested
that his feelings were sincere. The gesture has that
naïve bungling about it that is mixed up in all his
half-hearted attempts to justify himself. The Queen's
lips must have curled in disdain as she read the greeting
—she who had laid every evil at the feet of Orléans.

. . . . . .

Ever since his departure his friends in Paris had
urged him to come back if only to show that he was not
afraid of Lafayette. The inquiry which the High Court
of the Châtelet was holding had alarmed many of the
deputies. There was an air of mystery about it. Any
one of the revolutionaries felt they might be involved.
As the spring approached the death of the Emperor had
changed the political scene and Philippe's mission
appeared even less justified than before. He found that

every time he demanded instructions from Paris he was put off with vague assurances. He asked to be recalled, and Montmorin showed clearly in his reply that, mission or no mission, he intended to prevent his return.

The Feast of the Federation was at hand and Philippe, urged by Laclos and Biron, determined to be present. On June 25th he wrote to the King declaring that he intended to leave on July 3rd. Another letter was sent to La Touche to be read in the Assembly, announcing that he considered that his presence in London was no longer useful, and that his honour and his duty urged him to take his place again as a deputy and to be present at the reconciliation of all Frenchmen at the Feast of the Federation. Both the Court and Lafayette became hysterical. Montmorin wrote urgently saying that the return was most ill-advised, and Lafayette sent Bonneville a second time to threaten or scare the Duke into remaining. But Philippe showed surprising determination and refused to be impressed. He received Bonneville haughtily and replied that nothing but an order by the Assembly would delay his departure. The Assembly chose to see nothing more than a personal quarrel between the prince and Lafayette, and issued no order.

As usual, the clearest judgment on the whole situation came from Mirabeau, who was already devoting his genius to giving advice to the King— advice which was dearly paid for and consistently ignored. "The Duke of Orléans," wrote Mirabeau, "must either be treated just well enough so that he has no cause to complain or he must be reduced to nothing. His party is no more than a phantom and can only exist by support from the Jacobins . . . do not make a martyr out of him . . . The Duke is despised and incapable. What is there to fear from such a man? To serve him is to weaken him; to *ménager* is to kill him and his party. Then let him be well received at Court! This mark of the King's goodness will enchain him—his peace with the Court would prevent the Jacobins from claiming him. The fear of losing his domains in a complete upheaval will restrain him, and if Lafayette has one more embarrassment I don't see anything very bad in that."

Philippe arrived during the night of July 10th. The following day he appeared in the Assembly where he read a statement of his motives in an embarrassed tone of voice and ended by repeating the civil oath to the nation, the law and the King. Laclos had seen that the tribunes were well packed and the applause was considerable. That evening he paid a visit to the King. "The sight of him," wrote Ferrière "inspired a feeling of horror in all those who happened to be in the château. The women turned their backs, the men looked at him with a disdain that was provocative: the King and Queen received him coldly. His unexpected arrival spread alarm among a great number of citizens. Every one believed that the Duke had come to lend his name to some new crime. The most sinister rumours were circulated. All the wildest ideas of terror-stricken imaginations were exaggerated. It was said that a great popular movement was about to be aroused in Paris and the provinces; the nobles would be murdered and the aristocratic deputies massacred in the Champs de Mars; the crown snatched from Louis XVI. and the Duke of Orléans put on the throne."

The ghost of conspiracy was not laid, and as Philippe walked through the salons of the Tuileries after his interview, an officer of the guard, named de Goguelat, went up to him, seized him by the shoulder and pushed him towards the door saying, "Ah, there you are, blackguard! How dare you appear here!" The question of a duel immediately arose. M. de Goguelat remarked that if he received a challenge he would send his valet to fight. There was a meeting of Philippe's council at the Palais Royal to decide the question. Laclos and Sillery, both of them soldiers, were in favour of avenging the insult by action, but calmer judgment prevailed and no challenge was sent. Probably it was the wiser course. Philippe was bound to come out badly whether he fought or abstained. He was a deputy, and it was illegal for deputies to duel. This was generally, though not always, observed. Many of the nobles who were expert swordsmen, even if they were indifferent legislators, tried to rid themselves of their opponents by this convenient method and issued challenges upon the slightest provocation. Occasionally they were accepted. Barnave and Lameth both fought duels when they were deputies, whereas Mirabeau received dozens of challenges and refused them all until, he remarked, he had ceased being a representative of the nation, when he would whip the lot of them together if they still wanted to fight.

In Philippe's case people chose to see physical cowardice, and it is perhaps unfortunate that he did not knock M. de Goguelat about the ears. Especially as that swaggering gentleman was evidently trying to curry royal favour by his act. "It was believed at the time," wrote Bouillé, "that this violent proceeding had been suggested to him beforehand. In any case the Queen's interest was strong enough to make her recommend me to employ him later in the flight to Varennes."

Such was the end of the famous London mission, and such was Marie Antoinette's answer to the New Year greetings. Not only did it delight the courtiers, it delighted Philippe's followers, who had looked with dismay upon his retreat to London and his evident wish to make his peace with the Court. It gave them new assurance that that great source of action—the Orléans Treasury—would not be shut to their eager hands.

Mirabeau's wise advice had been completely ignored. Yet the hysterical fears that abounded were unjustified, for the great Feast of the Federation passed off peacefully and turned out to be a triumph for Lafayette and brotherly love. In fact, it was about the only peaceful occurrence in the Revolution. On July 14th the Duke of Orléans walked in the procession, wrote Mrs. Elliot, "and people were much surprised to see him after the reports that had been circulated.

"I saw him that same day. He dined with me, as did the Duc de Biron and others. The Duke expressed much regret at leaving England; would to God that he had stayed there."

CHAPTER XXV

PERSONAL WORLD

A FTER his return from London Philippe was more
than ever the political slave of Laclos. This sinister
and illusive figure seemed to fasten on him like a leech,
and Mme de Genlis had to admit temporary defeat at
the hands of her rival. To her, Philippe's departure
had been inconceivable from every point of view. Yet
this shrewd, ambitious woman was not without
resources. Her influence over his family life remained
more powerful than ever, and she was beginning to
transfer her political hopes from the father on to the
eldest son.

Difficult as it is for us to know that lost world,
remote as it is from us, with its red caps and aristocrats,
its mixture of old courtliness and wild slogans, yet the
passions of men and women remain the same, neither
old nor new. Philippe's love for his children was far
greater than his love for politics, and Mme de Genlis
with unerring instinct had made herself not only indispensable to their upbringing, but had established
herself so completely in their hearts that they regarded
her with a sort of adoration. She was their mama,
their dear friend, their counsellor and their guide.
"In truth," wrote the eldest, the Duc de Chartres, "in
truth, I don't know what I will become when I am no
longer with her." She had educated them demo-

cratically, " and it must be recognised that the young princes, Chartres, Montpensier and Beaujolais, were perfectly brought up." How democratic and how perfectly suited to the new world their education was is evident from the wide range of activities as well as the encyclopaedic intellectual training of Chartres. The young prince worked as a mason, a carpenter and a smith—he visited factories and his journal notes the days upon which he learned hospital work at the "Hôtel-Dieu." His manners were quiet and reserved, though he could, and often did, show enthusiasm for the new constitutional ideas. His morals were spartan; in fact, everything about him was in the strongest contrast to the Orléans heritage. He was a modern and extremely popular young prince. All this was according to Philippe's wish, and when one evening at dinner at Monceau Chartres expressed his desire to join the Jacobins, Philippe not only approved but arranged that Sillery should present him to the club the next day.

This was too much for the poor Duchess of Orléans. She had seen her children alienated from her by the influence of Mme de Genlis. For ten years she had suffered in a state of resignation and self-denial that is pathetic to contemplate. Her opinions were traditional, pious and diametrically opposed to those of her husband. She had had to endure the mortification of discovering that the woman she had cherished as a friend was her husband's mistress and then watch that woman absorb the affections of her children. Even now the mildness of her nature recoiled from a scene and she sat down to write her reproaches with a tenderness that seemed to know its own defeat even from the beginning. "You are right, my dear friend," she wrote, "it is better that we write. When one discusses an interesting subject with some one whom one loves one is apt to get heated." The first subject of discussion is naturally Mme de Genlis. "I don't want to go back over the past again, as I have already said to you—the wrongs with which I reproach Mme de Genlis exist and cannot be destroyed either by her journal or by anything she could say to you. I myself have seen and understood all that has displeased me. It is only concerning the future tha: makes me refer again to Mme de Genlis. She cannot justify herself but she can repair the wrong she has done."

Yet even now the Duchess did not ask for her dismissal. Her phrases are vague, tender and irresolute. "There remains," she continued, "an interesting subject upon which I want to talk to you and about which I want you to know how I feel. You will guess that Mme de Buffon is the subject in question. I confess that at the beginning of your liaison with her I was in despair. Accustomed as I was to your phantasies, I was frightened and profoundly affected when I saw you form a tie which could take away your confidence from me. Mme de Buffon's behaviour since you have formed the connection with her has made me reconsider the prejudices which I had against her. I have recognised that she has so true and so disinterested an attachment for you, and that her feeling for me is so perfect, that I cannot help being interested in her. It is impossible that some one who really loves you should have no rights over me—so she has some that are very real, and on this point you can be still quite at ease with me. I repeat it, my dear friend —what I should wish for—what would really make me happy is that you should be completely at your ease with me and then you should find in your wife a gentle companionship which would attract you and contribute to your happiness."

After this resigned admission she came at last to what touched her most at the moment—the desire of her son to join the Jacobins. It was against every instinct, every opinion that was natural to her; her respect for the Monarchy and all the traditions of the old régime, and her respect for the Pope and all the tenets of the Roman Church. She saw in it, quite rightly, the triumph of modern ideas over the minds of her children. She knew that Mme de Genlis had often taken them to the tribunes of the Jacobin club to listen to the debates. She had seen them, at Mme de Genlis's suggestion, appear in the uniform of the National Guard instead of the insignia of their royal birth. She had felt them growing indifferent towards herself and she had had to confess that she no longer counted in their lives. It is a broken-hearted letter. One can well imagine that Philippe did not even bother to read it through.

"If the Jacobins were only composed of deputies," she wrote, "they would be less dangerous because they would be known by their conduct in the Assembly and my son could be forewarned, but how is he to be put on his guard against the kind of people who form the majority and who are certainly able to mislead the opinions of a young man of seventeen? If my son were twenty-five, as I have told you, I would not be tormented, because he would be able to form his own judgment, but at seventeen, thrown with a society of this kind—really, my dear friend, that is not reasonable, it makes me regret that he has come out of the hands of Mme de Genlis."

Nothing that the Duchess wrote had the slightest effect. The young Duc de Chartres was presented and elected to the famous club on November 1st when he was received with loud applause. For a month he held the post of *censeur* or *huissier*, that is to say, he had to mind the door, introduce members and keep out non-members. He also had to expel those who started a fight or refused to quiet down, and to chase out the stray cats and dogs that wandered in by accident or design. "It was the reign of equality."

Philippe was delighted at his son's election. A week later the young *censeur* wrote in his journal, "Yesterday, my father sent for me and received me in an extremely good humour and gave me fifty louis. I gave ten of them to my brother."

The Duchess was utterly cast down at her failure to regain any influence over her husband or her children. Supported by one of her ladies-in-waiting, Mme de Castelleux (née Jenny Plunket), she made a desperate and futile attempt to break Mme de Genlis's influence. The governess played her cards with an ability that her opponents were far from possessing. Moreover,

PRINCE OF THE BLOOD

she held the winning hand. She was still immensely necessary to Philippe—not as a mistress; that position had long ago been willingly surrendered to Agnès Buffon—but as a friend whose ideas had united his children to him and upon whose judgment he had grown accustomed to rely.

The struggle then was for the minds of the children, and as they worshipped Mme de Genlis and adored their father, it was bound to be an unequal one from the start. The unhappy Duchess broke off relations with Mme de Genlis, refused to receive her at the Palais Royal or to come herself to Bellechasse. There was a hectic writing of letters, in which Philippe was evidently embarrassed at his wife's perfectly natural though tardy efforts. But Mme de Genlis was secure behind her knowledge that she had his support. She could say at any time to the Duchess, "M. d'Orléans controls the arrangements of his children and you would not take a step opposed to his wishes and therefore to your duty."

As though she knew the clever governess would adopt these tactics, the Duchess, driven to desperation, determined to demand her resignation. Mme de Genlis records the scene in her memoirs. "She came in brusquely, sat down, told me to be silent, and took a paper out of her pocket, telling me in a very imperious tone that she was going to declare her intentions to me. Then she at once proceeded to read in a loud voice and with great volubility the most surprising document in the world.

"She signified to me in this written statement that

217

considering our difference of opinion, I had no other course to take if I were an honourable woman than to go away without further delay."

Mme de Genlis appeared very resigned—almost injured. She promised to leave within a month. In spite of everything that Philippe could do or say she would not change her mind. Philippe was in consternation and Chartres was visibly affected by this family crisis. Mlle d'Orléans was in a continual state of nerves. In fact the governess could witness herself the incredible hold that she had upon the lives and feelings of the Orléans family. Philippe had several scenes with the Duchess, after one of which she left the Palais Royal during the first days of April and went to Eu where the unhappy woman allowed her friends to take the first legal measures for a petition of separation.

A fortnight later Mme de Genlis departed with her beautiful Pamela for Lyons, not however without covering her retreat. She left a letter for her dear child and pupil, Mlle d'Orléans. One or two sentences are most revealing.

"I have been treated," she wrote, "as they would not treat a servant-girl, since the Duchess of Orléans forbade me to go to the Palais Royal even with you. . . .

"The Duke of Orléans has not left you in ignorance as to the petition for a separation made by the Duchess of Orléans: terrible heartrending fears for you and your brothers. Thank heaven I am not even made the pretext for the last outbreak of the Duchess of Orléans. She insisted on my going away to-day; she came here by herself. It was in my room a month ago. So she has gained what she wanted. Our separation is very cruel, my very dear, dear friend. . . . "

Mlle d'Orléans had an attack of nerves. She became so ill that couriers were sent galloping after Mme de Genlis and Pamela—couriers, we can well believe, who were not unexpected. They must come back. The Princess has fallen into a decline. They came back at a full gallop.

"My care and affection," said Mme de Genlis, "soon restored her to health."

Curiously enough the *Correspondance Secrète* commented on this family drama in political terms. It was reported that Mme de Genlis and her Pamela had journeyed to Lyons in order to visit the Jacobin clubs of that neighbourhood. "They say that the eloquence of the mother and the beauty of the daughter have worked marvels and won many servant for Philippe Capet, who is hiding as far as he can under the mask of a Friend of the Constitution."

But the only marvel that Mme de Genlis had worked was to lose Philippe his wife and the Duchess her children!

CHAPTER XXVI

WHITE-WASHING

THE only method of justifying the rioting and murdering of October 5-6th was to take it out of the hands of the Orléanists and put it in the hands of the Revolution. Journalists began writing about the prompt and necessary expedition to Versailles. Mirabeau declared that the mob, which he dignified by the name of the Parisian army, had had the glory of speed in its conquest, wisdom of conduct in its movements, and gentleness of moderation after its victory! What a gentle sight must have been the bleeding heads of the massacred bodyguards preceding the royal procession to Paris!

Finally, on August 6th, the prosecutor of the Châtelet, Boucher d'Arce, laid his voluminous report on the table of the Assembly with the conclusion that there was sufficient proof for the arrest of Mirabeau and the Duke of Orléans. As the arrests could not be made unless the Assembly considered that the accusation against these two members was justified, a committe of inquiry was formed and a deputy named Chabroud appointed reporter. On October 2nd, nearly a year after the tragic day, Chabroud the white-washer, as he was afterwards called, delivered his report. In the interval the Jacobins and the Orléanists had been busy with propaganda. The Châtelet was represented as being the Queen's great Wash-house—it was said to be in the pay of the Court, which was not unlikely; its report was influenced by party spirit and thus not impartial—which was true: it was in reality attacking the Revolution. This last approach assured Chabroud's success. It is not necessary to give his speech in detail. It was inflated with a very poor sort of revolutionary rhetoric and relied almost entirely on confusing the issue. He declared that, having examined the report with the greatest care, he had come to the conclusion that their two colleagues in the Assembly who appeared to be implicated, were in fact free of all guilt. "There had been no plot, unless you could consider the report as a sort of plot against the Revolution. Examine the names of the witnesses. They seem to be a league formed from the debris of the old regime to attach to the new order of things."

The Abbé Maury, one of the ablest orators of the right, found no trouble in demolishing Chabroud's speech. According to him, the report of the Châtelet showed clearly that there had been a plot, but he made an important distinction. He could find nothing that could be used as evidence against Mirabeau but his conclusions were not so favourable to the Duke of Orléans. In other words, the royalists were offering peace to Mirabeau and at the same time giving him a chance to desert the Duke of Orléans. The matter of guilt was entirely secondary. If Mirabeau accepted this easy way out, he would in a sense be under obligation to the Right. It is characteristic of the man that he scorned help of such nature and welcomed the chance both to justify himself and to confound his enemies. His speech was masterly. He dealt one by one with the witnesses with skill and humour, finally giving an account to the part he played at the time of Philippe's departure for London. "I am accused," he cried, "of having counselled the Duke of Orléans not to depart for England. Well, what do you want to conclude from that?" He declared that he saw in the departure an arbitrary act on the part of Lafayette, and that he opposed it out of the principle of the inviolability of the members of the Assembly. He confessed to having made indignant remarks when he heard that the Duke had left, but again he asked, "What conclusion does that point to?—simply that I thought the departure was a mistake."

Philippe was not present during this debate. As usual, he left it to the others to speak for him. Generous as ever, Biron spoke in his defence with a chivalry that does him honour.

"I wish to confirm," he said, "the facts as stated by M. de Mirabeau, in which I am implicated. I knew nothing of the proposal submitted by M. de Lafayette to M. le Duc de Orléans till the moment when it was made, and M. d'Orléans had decided for himself. He gave me his confidence. I know his purity of purpose. I was deeply affected by the news. I feared that so great a sacrifice would be misinterpreted and that he would be accused of imaginary crimes which would have vanished in his presence, and therefore I opposed his departure. M. d'Orléans replied that he wished to give the King proof of the purity of his intentions;

that M. de Lafayette had told him that his name was being used to disturb the public peace. I still argued, but in vain. M. d'Orléans went."

"Allow me to make one single remark upon this amazing inquiry. Do we find on the lists of witnesses the name of one defender of liberty? Can we suppose that these would all have been silent if they had known who were guilty? In M. d'Orléans's name I pledge myself to furnish you with details which will prove his innocence of the charge and silence calumny."

It is reported that Biron walked from the tribune to his seat amid loud cheers. But unfortunately it is not reported that those important details about Philippe's innocence were ever forthcoming. Nevertheless the Assembly decreed that there was no case for conviction against either Mirabeau or the Duke of Orléans and the famous incident was closed, although Dumont and many others might still think that "the absolution of the Assembly is not the absolution of history and many veils yet remain to be raised before these events can be pronounced upon."

CHAPTER XXVII

COUP DE THÉÂTRE

DURING the spring and summer of 1791, Philippe tried persistently to rid himself of his political hangers-on. Yet during that time he came closer to wearing the Crown of France than at any other time. "I am sick of being the object of every kind of scandal and the pawn of every rogue that comes along," he wrote to Biron. And yet the rogues and the conspirators came nearer to realising their dream of a new dynasty with Orléans on the throne and themselves in the treasury than they ever would again. Philippe himself was the least enthusiastic about the whole thing. Since April he had been demanding active service as a general officer from M. Duportail, the Minister of War. Before considering the momentous events of this summer, a glance at this correspondence is necessary to throw some light upon Philippe's state of mind.

"M. de Biron told me," he wrote on April 5th to the Minister, "that you had said that the King had not included me in the list of general officers . . . I beg you to let me know if the King has given any reason for this refusal, because I here repeat the declaration I previously made to you that I feel no guilt whatever towards him. I know that in the eyes of many around him I am guilty of being a zealous partisan of the

224

THE DUKE AND DUCHESS OF CHARTRES AT HOME IN THE
PALAIS ROYAL, 1779

constitution and the Revolution—but this cannot be a wrong, either in the King's eyes or in yours. Pray give me the explanation I ask for as soon as possible."

Duportail's reply was evasive. The King would decide nothing positive yet. As a matter of fact the Minister had included Philippe's name in the original army list, but he told Biron that the King had struck it off and that his resistance was too strong to overcome.

Philippe persisted. He was willing to serve even in a subordinate position to Bouillé or Rochambeau. On August 16th he informed the Minister that he had spoken personally to every member of the military committe of the Assembly and that he had met with no opposition. His letter has an unaccustomed dignity about it. "As a relation of the King," he wrote, "I cannot pretend to any preference but neither can I renounce the rights which every citizen has to justice. You, sir, at this moment, alone choose the general officers. I persist in demanding to be employed as such. I await your reply with impatience."

Duportail answered the following day, saying that nothing could be altered. "It would not be convenient," he wrote, "considering your position *vis-à-vis* the King, to employ you without his consent and to profit by the short time that His Majesty will remain absent from the details of the administration to make a choice which he has already refused."

On August 17th Philippe wrote again, demanding what the Minister implied by his phrase "*vis-à-vis* the King" and pointing out that the Assembly had decreed the very day following the Minister's last letter that the King's relatives were only under the common law. "The actual circumstances," he added, "are very different from those at the time when you said that I had met with the King's refusal which you are bringing against me now."

On that same day, August 17th, the Minister replied in a curt note reiterating his refusal because of Philippe's relationship to the King.

Now this correspondence is not only interesting in itself as evidence of Philippe's desire to get out of politics into action but it is doubly interesting when the dates are examined. Between April 12th, when the first letter was written, to the evening of August 17th, when Duportail repeated his refusal, the Revolution had advanced by leaps and bounds. On June 21st, the King and the Royal Family had fled and had been captured at Varennes and brought back to Paris. The dream of Laclos seemed within an ace of being realised. Yet on July 17th, one month before the last two letters were written, Lafayette had blown it to Kingdom Come in what became known as the Massacre of the Champs de Mars.

Throughout these events "Orléanism was an intrigue rather than a party." It appears consistently as an anarchic force, yet Philippe himself is almost indistinguishable. Where we do find him he is acting in a manner very unlike the leader of a conspiracy— a manner which must have caused acute distress to Laclos, Sillery, Danton, Marat and all the others who used his name and lived on his money.

It is not unlikely that the mob which prevented the

royal family from going to celebrate Easter at St. Cloud on April 18th was organised with the express purpose of forcing the King to escape and thus create a state of emergency. Certainly the riot was organised by Danton, and many known Orléanists were noticed among the crowd. Philippe's actions cannot be traced on that April day, but a week later Fersen, the lover of the Queen, wrote, "It is believed that the faction of the Duke of Orléans is the cause of what has happened, for the chiefs of the Jacobins are with good reason very annoyed." This also indicates that the Court realised a division between Orléanists and Jacobins. Certainly on the road to Varennes Marie Antoinette believed that she and the King were fleeing from murderers in the pay of the Duke of Orléans.

It is not surprising that Orléanism had attracted an increasing number of followers during this spring and summer. Political morality, with few exceptions, did not exist. The highest bidder got the most followers. Corruption and intrigue were the rule, not the exception. The possibility of the King's flight was a constant source of alarm, and it was evident to all the political riff-raff that in this event the Duke of Orléans stood an excellent chance of being Regent, perhaps King, and the founder of a new dynasty. To flatter his son Chartres, who was an engaging young man, and to keep close to Philippe's chief councillors, was then no more than practical politics. You might despise the man, but it might happen that his opponent would not be strong enough to prevent his being swept into power. And in that case it was as well to be on good terms with those about him.

Laclos in particular was working on this supposition. He had been elected to the Jacobin Club after his return from London, and from that vantage point he acted as the chief of the correspondence committee by which the society extended its influence and maintained its power throughout the country. It is not the purpose of this book to examine the activities of the famous club which became the nerve centre of the Revolution and the organiser of the Terror. It was a far greater and more terrible force than Orléanism, especially when, after 1792, it became imbued with a fanatical spirit of savage virtue that turned men into mystical murderers. But during the summer of 1791 it is certain that many members of the club, Danton in particular, were deep in the Orléanist intrigue, and many others were keeping a watchful eye on Orléanist possibilities.

The story of the flight to Varennes and the return to the Tuileries is one of the immortal stories of history. On the morning of June 21st France could have been had for the asking—instead of which the country was merely salvaged for a moment by Lafayette and the Assembly. Once again there is a touch of the ridiculous about the tragic picture. The King and Queen were fleeing from Orléanist murderers. Everything seemed to have happened according to the designs of the conspirators. Now assuredly they would burst upon the scene with new banners and shouting. The streets were thronged with a people that seemed stunned and only awaited a leader. The throne was abandoned. It was the moment when the arch-conspirator, the dreaded Duke of Orléans, clad in the uniform of the huzzars, would appear on horseback, declare the flight of the King signified abdication, and put himself at the head of the country amid a rising torrent of enthusiasm. Instead of which Philippe, dressed in English clothes of the latest fashion, got into a cabriolet, and drove smiling about Paris, receiving some desultory applause from a bewildered populace.

Meanwhile at the Jacobins, Danton attacked Lafayette with sanguinary violence, demanding his head and accusing him of treason to the country for having helped the King to escape. It was the usual Orléanist method of throwing the guilt attributed to them upon their opponents. Lafayette, the great opposer of Orléanism, must be got rid of first. The hall was crowded, and wild applause greeted every burst of Danton's invective. "The General promised to prevent the King's escape or answer for it with his head. We demand that he keep his promise." Suddenly the door opened, and three hundred deputies of the National Assembly entered—Lafayette arm in arm with Alexander Lameth, followed by Barnave, Duport and the rest. News had been brought to the Assembly that Danton would attempt to start a violent movement in favour of the Duke, and with a promptness, dignity and courage which were admirable in every way, the entire Left had accompanied Lafayette to face this new danger. Danton attempted to carry the mutiny with a high hand. He failed completely, and when at the end of a vigorous speech Barnave not only vindicated Lafayette but cried, "L'Assemblée Nationale, voilà notre guide: la Constitution, voilà notre cri de ralliement," the entire meeting, with the exception of a handful of Orléanists, arose cheering, and filed back to the Assembly with the deputies. The needed gesture had been made, but Philippe had not made it.

Yet his friends were not discouraged. Laclos, cautious and secretive as ever, had actually chosen the day after the King's arrest became known to have Philippe presented to the Jacobin Club. The minutes of June 23rd contained the following information:

"M. d'Orléans, presented by M. de Monspensier and seconded by five members, begs the Assembly to abridge the form of reception in his case because of his desire to be admitted to the society." There was some opposition to this, but M. Dubois de Crancé swept it aside by saying that members of the National Assembly only needed to be introduced in order to be made members.

Immediately after Philippe had taken his seat, Laclos spoke from the tribune. He said there were three urgent questions for discussion—the departure of the King, the arrest of the King, the return of the King. The departure of the King had only served to show the imposing picture of the behaviour of the people of Paris. The King's arrest had shown that the conduct of the provinces was equal to that of Paris. There remains the return of the King. "For thirty-six hours," said Laclos, "I have reflected upon what course the Assembly should adopt, and I confess ingenuously that my reflections have as yet led me nowhere. I demand that this question be made the order of the day."

In the debate which followed a member, whose name is not given, but who undoubtedly was a deputy, declared that although the King had committed a crime, he had not abdicated his throne. "Beware of private interests," he cried. "Their influence is terrible against liberty." This attitude, which was precisely the attitude the National Assembly was preparing to adopt, was violently attacked by Danton, who saw in it the end of the Orléanist schemes. "L'Individu royal," he cried, "ne peut plus être roi dès qu'il est imbécile. . . . It is not a regent that is needed: it is a council of interdiction."

All the newspapers discussed the question, and its is interesting to notice that the idea of a republic was highly unpopular. Several editors, such as Carra and Gorsa, favoured a regency. One, named Perlet, in a paper called *L'Assemblée Nationale*, suggested a great petition to establish it by popular acclamation. This idea began to gain supporters. Perlet's article was hailed as an Orléanist manifesto, and during the week, June 21st to 27th, the Jacobin meetings became more and more occupied with the question.

Yet underneath this feverish activity it was evident that something was happening which was contrary to Orléanist designs. On the 27th Cambon returned to Danton's idea of a council of regency. But he gave it a very definite meaning. "One of the previous speakers," he said, "pretends that this Council must have a leader to give it power of action. But have not the administrative councils and the courts of justice the power of necessary action through the president which they chose themselves? Besides, what princes are there of this family (the Bourbons) whose conduct could inspire you into enough esteem to confide such great power to them? As for me, I don't know a single one." This remark was applauded. Not a single voice was heard in Philippe's favour. At the end of the session another member also insisted on a council of regency, but without a regent at its head. Moreover, he made the unexpected announcement that "the Prince, whose rank would have given him that right, will not accept it," and that "a declaration by this Prince will appear to-morrow in the *Journal de Paris*, announcing with this renunciation the price which this Prince attached to the title of French citizen."

On June 28th the following letter addressed to Perlet appeared in the Paris papers:

"Having read in your issue No. 689[1] your opinion as to the steps to be taken after the return of the King, and all that your justice and impartiality dictate in my regard, I must repeat what I have already publicly declared on the 21st and 22nd of this month, to several members of the National Assembly—namely, that I am ready to serve my country on land, on sea, in the diplomatic service—in

[1] L'Assemblée Nat. No. 692. June 28-91.

232

a word, in any position that requires unbounded zeal and devotion to the public welfare; but that if it is a question of governing, I renounce now and forever the right the constitution gives me."

The letter ended with a fervent eulogy of national liberty and was signed "Louis Philippe d'Orléans." This direct counter-blast to Laclos, at the very moment when everything appeared to favour his schemes, had been composed by Mme de Genlis, who had watched the political scene with grave misgivings. "I imagine," she wrote ingenuously, "that he (Philippe) got me to draw up this declaration because the recognised councillors did not approve their steps which ambition could neither suggest nor find prudent."

It was a considerable triumph for the governess over her rival. The older influence in Philippe's life and his own indifference to ambition had gained ascendance at ths critical moment.

Yet Laclos refused to acknowledge defeat. Philippe's renunciation had not killed the idea of a popular petition, and Laclos might well think that he would not be able to stand firm against a great wave of enthusiasm. During the early morning of the 16th a petition composed by Laclos and Brissot was drawn up at the Jacobins after a tumultuous session. The abdication of the King was demanded, and "his replacement by constitutional means." This implied that the dauphin would be proclaimed King and the Duke of Orléans Regent. But when this petition was carried to the Champ de Mars and about to be laid on the altar of the country with much pomp and fustian, another voice was suddenly heard proclaiming: "No more Kings!" The Orléanists' phrase was repudiated and a new phrase written in its place: "The French people will never recognise Louis XVI. for their King, nor any other person."

At the same time the Assembly declared the inviolability of the King, thus making the petition hors de lois.

Yet in spite of this the agitators were determined to present their demand for dethronement. The rest is well known. Lafayette and Bailly turned out with the Guard. The Riot Act was read. A few people were killed on the Champ de Mars. But what is not so well known is that it was Mme. de Genlis who warned Bailly that the new petition was being prepared. She sent her husband, one of Philippe's most intimate friends, with the message that was responsible for smashing Laclos's dreams into atoms. The chief agitators disappeared into their bolt holes. The Jacobins scattered like scared rabbits as soon as they heard the news, rushing out of the doors, even climbing out of the windows, to the jeers of the onlookers. Laclos resigned from the club. Danton fled to England, and five months later Philippe was made Admiral of France.

The great conspiracy had failed. What would have happened had it succeeded? Louis XVI. replaced by the young dauphin, Louis XVII., with Philippe as regent? Chateaubriand and many others have asked the same questions. Would it have been a happy compromise between the revolution and the old régime? It is impossible to think so unless we suppose the chief characters involved to be very different from what they were.

Not until 1830 did such an idea find form in reality, and then, by the curious irony of history, it was Lafayette, the great opposer of Orléanism from '89-'92, whose immense influence was the deciding factor in placing the son of Philippe Égalité on the throne of Louis XVI., as Louis Philippe I., King of the French.

CHAPTER XXVIII

ADMIRAL OF FRANCE

DURING the summer of 1791 the Revolution appeared to have come to an end. The constitution was completed and accepted by the King. The great majority of the people believed that they were about to enjoy the inestimable happiness of their new liberties. For the moment Orléanism was as dead as last year's news. Philippe himself viewed the new order of things with optimism. "Everything here is going marvellously," he wrote to his son, the Duc de Chartres, on September 18th. "The funds have gone up a little. The King's acceptance (of the Constitution) is proclaimed everywhere. There will be a lot of dances and illuminations, cannons and drums, no church ceremonies."

He was present at the historic closing session of the Estates, and wrote that evening, September 20th, to his son: "I am writing to you from the Jacobins and from my seat as secretary. This morning the King came to perform the ceremony of closing the Assembly. He made a speech which was perfectly composed. The president, who was Thouret, replied to him with one equally perfect, and the King left to the applause of the entire hall. He announced that he was about to signify to all the foreign powers his acceptance of the Constitution. After his departure the minutes of to-day's session were read, and when that was done the president said, 'The National Assembly has terminated its sessions,' and we all went out. There is all the news I have to send you."

On October 11th Mme de Genlis had taken Philippe's daughter, Mlle Orléans, and Pamela to England, accompanied by Petion, who was about to be elected Mayor of Paris, and by Voidel, an ex-deputy and friend of Philippe, later to be his defender before Fouquier-Tinville. This journey has been the subject of wild speculations. Even at the time the *Correspondance Secrète* wrote that "the new plan which hovers over Republicanism consists in the event of the deposition of Louis XVI., in calling to the throne a son of the King of England, on the condition that he upholds the Revolution against those who wish to destroy it. It seems that this project was the reason for the journey that M. Pétion made to England, when he consulted with the Society of Friends of the Revolution" (the English Jacobins). The idea, apparently, was to marry Mademoiselle to the Duke of York, who would then be in a position to be called to the throne of France. This fantastic scheme, which the journalist Carra actually mentioned in the Jacobins, appears never to have been mentioned either to Philippe or to the Duke of York; and when George III. heard of it he snorted with indignation.

.   .   .   .

On December 18th, 1791, Philippe was made Admiral of France. This "very remarkable promotion" was due to the outgoing Minister of Marine,

M. Thévenard, who had hurried on the affair because, as he told his successor, Bertrand de Moleville, he believed that the nomination of the Duke of Orléans to the rank of Admiral would ensure the King a sufficient degree of popularity to enable him to keep the new Assembly[1] in proper bounds.

Nothing could be more revealing than Bertrand's account of Philippe's reactions to his promotion.

"The Duke of Orléans," wrote the new Minister of Marine, "was not satisfied with writing to me that he had accepted the rank of Admiral: he paid me a visit as well, and among other matters he assured me that he set a high value on the favour which the King had conferred upon him, because it gave him means of convincing His Majesty how much his sentiments had been calumniated." This declaration was made with an air of great openness and sincerity and accompanied with the warmest protestations of loyalty. "I am very unfortunate," he said, "without deserving to be so. A thousand atrocities have been laid to my charge of which I am completely innocent. I have been supposed guilty by many merely because I have disdained to justify myself from crimes of which I have a real horror. You are the first minister to whom I ever said as much, because you are the only one whose character ever inspired me with confidence. You will soon have an opportunity of judging whether my conduct gives the lie to my words."

"He pronounced these words with a voice and

[1] The Legislative Assembly which had succeeded the Constituent or National Assembly.

manner which convinced me that he meant them as an answer to the air of incredulity with which I listened to him. I answered him that I was so much afraid of weakening the force of his expressions in reporting them to the King that I begged him to deliver them himself to His Majesty. He replied that it was precisely what he wished, and that if he could flatter himself that the King would receive him he would go to Court next day.

"That same evening I gave His Majesty an account of the visit I had received from the Duke of Orléans and all that had passed, adding that I could not help being convinced of the sincerity of his professions. The King resolved to receive him, and the following day had a conversation with him for more than half an hour, with which His Majesty seemed well satisfied.

"'I agree with you,' he said to me, 'that he returns to us sincerely, and will do everything he can to repair the mischief that has been done in his name—and in which quite possibly he has not had as great a share as we suspected.'"

Every word of this account rings true. The ex-minister, M. Thévenard, had performed a master stroke by making Philippe an admiral. His vanity and pride were satisfied, his rancour against the Queen was assuaged, his sense of frustration wiped out, his desire for action aroused, and his hereditary sense of form was flattered. In fact, the past troubles might have ended in a peaceful understanding.

This happy state of affairs lasted less than a week.

The Sunday following his interview with the King—it is Bertrand who records it—"the Duke of Orléans came to the King's *lever*, where he met with the most mortifying reception from the courtiers, who were ignorant of what had passed, and from the royalists, who usually came on that day to pay their court to the royal family. They pressed round him, purposely treading on his toes and pushing him towards the door. When he went into the Queen's apartment, where the cloth was already laid, they cried out as soon as he appeared, ' Let nobody come near the dishes,' insinuating that he might throw poison in them.

"The insulting murmurs which his presence excited forced him to withdraw without having seen any of the royal family. He was followed by the courtiers to the top of the stairs, and as he was going down some of them spit over the staircase on him. He hurried out, filled with rage and indignation and convinced that the King and Queen were the authors of these outrages, of which they were not only ignorant but extremely concerned when they were informed."

From that moment the Duke of Orléans conceived implacable hatred and vowed vengeance against the King and Queen. He kept his oath but too well. "I happened to be at Court on that day," wrote Bertrand, "and was an eye-witness to the scene I have just related."

CHAPTER XXIX

VOLUNTEER

SINCE the declaration of war on April 20th, Philippe had renewed his request to be employed in active service, and again he had been refused. Finally the King had shrugged his shoulders and said, "Let him go where he wants to."

His two eldest sons were with the Army of the North, and Philippe determined to join them. His letters during May show how anxious he was to get away from Paris. "I am only kept here by the passport that I want to have from the Minister of Marine," he wrote, "which will state clearly that I am going nowhere except to the army of Rochambeau, and that I have the agreement of these gentlemen. They say that all the troops will be sent into camp somewhere, but where I don't know. When you know the place, I want you to look for a little house for me at the gates of their camp, as I told you before. I will go there and spend the time near you and my friend Biron very pleasantly until I am employed, and I will march with you as an amateur if you march on the enemy again, as I hope. I have always decided to do that, as you know, and if I hadn't decided I would now without any doubt, for it's impossible to stay here and support the joy of the aristocrats and the lamentations of false patriots. I will send my cook on

Saturday by the Valenciennes coach, with some linen
and a part of my things."

"Dumouriez, the Foreign Minister, approves my
resolution, and tells me that, once having left, he will
find means to employ me agreeably. We'll see whether
he is right or not. Show my letter to Biron and ask
his advice about what I have to do when I arrive,
because I have quite decided not to stay here, and I
don't see where else I could go. Good-day, my dear
friends. I won't have Laclos or any other secretary
with me."

Another letter mentions again Dumouriez's
promise to find him a post which would be agreeable.
"I doubt if they will find me one," commented
Philippe, "for I have no great desire to be employed;
but I want it well proved that it is not on account of
laziness nor heedlessness nor fear. Once I have proved
all these things I will retire perfectly tranquilly with
the greatest pleasure, especially if one is able to travel
every now and then. . . . Adieu, mon cher enfant,
je t'aime de tout mon coeur. . . . Show my letter to
Biron."

During May this correspondence continued, and
Philippe arranged to take a house for Madame de
Buffon in a town near the camp, though for himself
he wrote that he much preferred *les maisons de
campagne*. On May 15th he added an interesting bit
of news:

"It is believed in Paris that there will be a lot of
trouble here in a few weeks, or that the King will go.
That would be a bad thing because of the intentions of

the King of Prussia, which I wrote to you about the other day."

On the 25th he wrote: "It is not believed that the King will refuse his sanction to the decree passed yesterday concerning the priests. It is excellent. I think that whatever is done, everything will be calm here."

In the beginning of June he went to join his sons with the Army of the North. Rochambeau had been replaced by Luckner, whom Philippe called "bon patriote." His greatest friend, Biron, was commanding a division. Philippe himself joined as a volunteer without rank. It was a strange gesture—not without a certain greatness about it, if such a term can be applied to overcoming a sense of frustration. The first prince of the blood, Admiral of France, unable to find employment, joined up in the ranks of an army in which his son was a colonel, soon to be promoted to the rank of Lieutenant-General.

Luckner's acceptance of this new recruit was dated "June 5th, Valenciennes. M. d'Orléans having communicated to me the letters of the Minister which authorises him on behalf of the King to serve as volunteer in the Army of the North, I give my consent with the greatest pleasure to an action which sets so good an example."

But it was in vain that Philippe tried to obliterate himself from the political scene. When you have the biggest income in the country, three thousand creditors who are very interested in everything you do, a title which symbolises opposition, and a multitude of suckers stuck on your keel, it is not easy to sail away into a happy anonymity.

The very day after Luckner had signed the acceptance for the new volunteer, the official *Moniteur* reported a remarkable outburst in the session of the National Assembly in Paris. A deputy named Ribès had made a violent attack on Philippe. His speech was exactly like all anti-Orléanist declarations: wild, irresponsible and unsupported by proof. He ended by demanding a decree of accusation against Philippe, Dumouriez and Bonnecarère, a friend of the General's. His tirade had been frequently interrupted. It seems upon reading it as though M. Ribès represents that state of fear, amounting to a conspiracy complex, which obsessed so many Frenchmen, and which did as much to create panic as the agitators themselves. Ribés's opinion was that the so-called Austrian Committee which was supposed to be composed of Marie Antoinette, Count Mercy, the Austrian Ambassador, Montmorin, Bertrand de Moleville, in fact almost any one whom the patriots wanted to accuse, was in reality nothing but the Orléans faction in disguise. This committee was credited with all sorts of malicious schemes, chief among which was the idea of enlisting foreign help to put down the Revolution. Other interesting assertions were made by Ribès. The frequent trips of M. Orléans and Talleyrand to London proved to him that there must be a plot to give up the French colonies to England. The speech has that same wild spirit of fear, that same obsession with plots and disasters that the Russian political scene has presented lately with such bloody results. It could serve as a model of how not to speak in public. It is inspired by a form of mania even more inherent in modern political life than in the Convention; the mania of disaster, fed with panic and vomited from the throat of every petty demagogue or powerful dictator. Ribés was frequently interrupted. Members cried out that his speech was the result of an imagination in delirium. Guadet, a leading Girondist, treated it with disdain mixed with political sense. "Among the calumnies you have just heard," he said, "I have noticed three in particular: (1) That against the English nation at the moment when we can hope for an alliance with her; (2) the distrust that the speaker has tried to cast upon M. Talleyrand; (3) the imputations made regarding M. Louis Philippe, Prince Français. I do not call for the severity of the Assembly upon the conduct of M. Ribès. On the contrary I demand that the Assembly, considering his opinion as an act of delirium, should pass to the order of the day."

Another deputy, M. Gossier, rose and declared that he thought Ribés was mad, and Guadet's motion was carried. But the time was not far off when the entire country would be in the grip of that same madness of suspicion, denunciation and revenge.

The allusion to Talleyrand and Philippe at this moment was pertinent, for Talleyrand was in London seeking to negotiate the treaty which Philippe had failed to bring about. It must have been during these early days in June while he was preparing to join his sons that Philippe made a hurried trip to London.

Dumont, Mirabeau's friend, recalls having seen him at Ranelagh one warm, lovely evening. The strange scene is worth pausing over. Dumont had been dining with the new Ambassador, Chauvelin. After dinner the party went on to Ranelagh, which was then the last word in fashion. "It is," wrote Dumont, "a large round room with alcoves opening out of it like boxes in a theatre, and the orchestra in the centre. One strolls around and around or stops in the alcoves to get refreshments. At our arrival we heard almost at once, 'Here is the French Embassy.' Curious looks, but of a curiosity not at all benevolent, were turned from every side upon our battalion, for we were eight or ten persons. Soon we could feel that we would have a free passage in which to walk about, for every one drew back to left and right as we approached, as though they were afraid to be caught in some contagious atmosphere. The battalion became more and more noticeable as an emptiness formed around it. One or two courageous people came to greet M. de Chauvelin or M. de Talleyrand. A moment later we saw a man wandering about entirely by himself, who was avoided for other reasons. It was the Duke of Orléans, whom people fled from with particular care."

This solitary apparition does not appear again on the English scene.

Philippe was with the Army on June 20th, when the mob invaded the Tuileries. When he heard of it he wrote to Grace Elliot telling her how glad he was to be out of Paris at that moment, and adding: "I hope they will not now accuse me." Mrs. Elliot's only remark was: If he was innocent, his friends perhaps were not. For her, the whole Revolution was expressed in one word: "horrid." And the famous invasion of the Tuileries by Santerre's murderous mob is described in a few sentences. "The Queen was frightened," she wrote, "and came and placed herself by the King's side, to whom she always fled for protection. They (the mob) brought a little red cap for the dear little dauphin."

During July the National Assembly had declared the country in danger and had ordered all civil and military functionaries to their posts. Philippe wrote at once to the Minister of Marine asking that gentleman to indicate his post as Admiral of France.

There seemed at last to be a chance of being employed in his own rank. While waiting for the Minister's reply he obtained leave to come to Paris. Once again the reply contained a refusal. The Minister wrote, saying that His Majesty had noticed the zeal with which he had shown in service for the State, but that it did not appear necessary to His Majesty to impose any new obligations upon him. Philippe prepared to return to the Army. But on July 27th the following note was handed to him from his eldest son:

"Monsieur le Mareschal Luckner has ordered me to tell you that the King has forbidden him to allow any volunteers to follow the Army who have not received a written permission signed by himself. He has ordered me to express all his regrets."

Another letter from Biron brought the same news: "I must inform you," it ran, "without loss of time, that M. le Mareschal Luckner has forbidden me to receive you with the Army of the Rhine without a letter from the King."

Once more shut out from action, Philippe wrote a long memorandum to the Assembly on August 2nd, presenting his case and quoting the letters he had received. At the end he stated that he wanted to be employed, as he had a right to be, in the Navy, and begged the Assembly to decree that the Minister should assign all officers to their posts. "It seems impossible," he wrote, "that there should exist public functionaries without functions and especially without posts."

The Assembly, overwhelmed with state business, listened to the memorandum and referred it to the Naval Committee, where it was lost in some pigeon-hole or other.

It is not altogether strange that Philippe, standing at a window of the Palais Royal, watched the fall of the Monarchy on the 10th of August with a certain indifference.

CHAPTER XXX

MELODRAMA

THE name of Orléans is lost in the bloody tumult of August 10th. Perhaps Danton and Marat may have entertained some hope of making Philippe king during the days that followed. If they did, it was short-lived, for on September 21st the National Convention decreed that royalty was abolished forever in France (a characteristically exaggerated and hopeful measure which was frantically applauded).

High up among the newly-elected members on the president's left, soon to be known as the Mountain, sat Philippe, last elected of the Parisian deputies, no longer bearing the proud name of Louis Philippe d'Orléans, but that of citizen Philippe Égalité. "I have no doubt," wrote Garat, "that he would have preferred to be on a rock in Norway."

Between August 10th and September 21st a great deal had happened to him. He had had the very doubtful distinction of being praised by Marat, who publicly begged fifteen thousand francs from him on September 2nd, the first day of the appalling massacres in the prisons. The *Ami du Peuple* had been the chief organiser of this butchery. His pamphlet, which was stuck up all over Paris on the morning of September 2nd, was full of cringing impudence. "As I don't like to waste my time in boot-licking," it read, "I here and now break with Roland and address myself to you, Louis Philippe of Orléans—you whom the heavens have overwhelmed with fortune's gifts, you with whom the nation shares the soul of a simple citizen. In the actual state of affairs you can only preserve your welfare in company with the *sans-culottes*. . . . In the name of the country, assist to-day in the propaganda of the light necessary to public welfare, by furnishing the *Ami du Peuple* the means of publishing his works without delay. The modest sum of fifteen thousand francs will suffice for the purchase of paper and wages for the workmen."

Philippe might well look with greater misgivings upon his new friends than upon his old enemies at Court.

On September 3rd, the day following Marat's pamphlet, there is a glimpse of him, for which we are indebted to Grace Elliot. This young Scotchwoman was as courageous as she was beautiful—and she was very beautiful. She was also devoted to Philippe, though she made no secret of the fact that she abhorred his politics and loved royalty. She had a house in the rue Miromesnil and another small country house at Meudon, outside the city barriers. Her money was invested in Philippe's estates and undoubtedly was provided by him. There is no evidence to show how intimate he was with her at this time, but he frequently went to dine or to breakfast with her.

On the night of September 2nd, the first night of the dreaded domiciliary visits, she had hidden at risk of her life the governor of the Tuileries, M. de Champsenets, whom the patriots were particularly anxious to find. He had distinguished himself by his vain attempts to prevent the pillage of the Château on August 10th, and had only escaped being butchered by lying for hours in the scorching sun, immovable, among the mutilated bodies of the Swiss Guard. Since August 10th he had taken refuge at the house of an English lady named Mrs. Meyler, who had sent to ask Grace Elliot's help when she heard of the approaching visits. Champsenets, and any one found giving him help, would have been instantly arrested and executed.

Mrs. Elliot said at once that she would do her best to help him. After trying in vain to get past the city barriers to her house at Meudon with Champsenets disguised as her servant, she took him to her house in the rue Miromesnil. It was late at night, and as the dreaded patrol approached, she hid Champsenets between the thick mattresses of her bed on the side next to the wall. At four o'clock in the morning a band of forty men entered and ransacked the house, running their bayonets through sofas, pillows and feather beds. To prevent them examining her own bed in the same thoughtful manner, Mrs. Elliot got into it herself. She had ordered her servant to light all the candles in the big chandeliers, and when the uncouth brigands burst in they were taken aback by the sight of the beautiful young woman lying in her big bed in a blaze of light. After a moment's hesitation they ransacked the room, opening cupboards, sticking their bayonets into sofas and rapping on the walls to discover secret hiding-places. One of them came up to the bed and ran his bayonet into the lower part of the mattress. When they had finished with the rest of the room they paused and stood looking at the figure on the bed. Several of them ordered her to get up, but French chivalry now played an odd prank. "One of them, less hard than the others, said there was no occasion to take me out of bed, as I could not dress before so many men." It was a close thing, though, and when finally they left Champsenets was almost unconscious with fear and suffocation and Mrs. Elliot had violent hysterics.

The next morning Philippe, on his way to his house at Monceau, noticed that the gates of Mrs. Elliot's house were open, and came in. He was in very low spirits. She told him about the visit of the patrol, but not about Champsenets. Philippe had particular reason to dislike the man. He had been among those courtiers who had formed the insulting crowd during his last visit to the Tuileries.

The following morning, September 4th, Philippe came to breakfast before eleven o'clock. He was still in very low spirits. And for a terrible reason. The day before the Princess de Lamballe had been butchered by a gang of assassins led by an Italian named Rotondo. Philippe had been dining at the Palais Royal with Agnès Buffon and some English friends when there was a tumult outside. Walking to the window, he had seen the severed head carried on the end of a pike and had contemplated it "coldly," says Montjoie, while Agnès Buffon half fainted, exclaiming: "My

God! My head will be paraded like that one day!"
And one of the Englishmen, overcome by horror, left
the room. This hideous murder was laid at Philippe's
door by several contemporary writers such as Montjoie,
Maton de la Varenne, and Peltier, who says that he
heard Rotondo boast of the murder later at a London
tavern. Rotondo and his band were supposed to be
in Orléanist pay. Therefore politicians like Manuel
and Fauchet concluded that the murder was planned
by Philippe. Manuel had actually been bribed to save
the Princess's life, and would probably have done so
if he had been allowed to. He could be humane if
he were well enough paid for it.

The motives for the murder were generally believed
to have been two: first, Philippe hoped to inherit the
dowry which was part of his father-in-law's fortune.
This, however, has been proved to be a comparatively
small sum, and can scarcely be taken seriously.
Secondly, the Princess, who had previously been
on the friendliest terms with Philippe (her husband's
brother-in-law), had, since the events of October
5th and 6th, refused to have anything more to do with
him, and not only had remained an intimate friend
of the Queen, but had shown a great deal of sympathy
with the Duchess of Orléans. Because of this it is
asserted that Philippe planned this horrible revenge.
Those are briefly the facts and the supposed motives
concerning this most bestial assassination of one who
had played no part amid all the agitations. "Nothing,"
wrote the revolutionary Mercier, "could render her
suspect in the eyes of the people, by whom she was only

known by innumerable acts of benevolence." It is a fearful charge to bring against any one, and Philippe's enemies have thrown it on to the huge pile of infamy which they have heaped above his memory. Like many others, it is entirely based on suppositions and rumours, unproved and unconvincing, except to those who are convinced even before any examination of the evidence.

But unproved though it must remain, either one way or the other, it is impossible not to take into account Philippe's actions on September 4th in estimating his spirit of revenge and the probability that he would resort to assassination out of personal rancour. As he came into Grace Elliot's drawing-room on that morning he was about to have the life of a man who had publicly and shamefully insulted him placed in his hands. Moreover, he could easily have accomplished his destruction and have made it seem a patriotic act to the popular party.

Mrs. Elliot wrote that she began the conversation by expressing sympathy for the members of the royal family who were locked up in "the horrid Temple." Philippe remarked that he was sure they would not be sorry for him if he were in a worse situation.

"I then told the Duke," says Mrs. Elliot, "in as quiet a manner as I could what I had done. He seemed much surprised and assured me that I should be found out; that I was in great danger; and that most certainly if Champsenets did not get, by some means or other, out of Paris he would be taken, and that both he and I would be executed.

"I then entreated him to get Champsenets out of Paris or to suffer him to be hid in his house at Monceau. The Duke assured me that such a place was impossible; that all his servants were spies from the Jacobin Club and that the part of the tower wall to which I alluded was surrounded by troops: in short, he saw no way of his getting away. . . .

"He asked me where I concealed him. I said, in the roof of my house, as I did not wish the Duke to know that he had heard our conversation. He told me I had exposed my life for a very bad purpose, for that Champsenets was a good-for-nothing creature; that many better people had been taken up and executed; that he wished I had saved somebody else, and that it would be cruel if I were to lose my life for such a poor, miserable being."

Mrs. Elliot wanted him to see Champsenets, but Philippe said it would be very imprudent. "Then, looking at his watch, he said he must go directly to the Convention, that he was then nearly an hour late . . . that he would see what he could do to get this man out my house, but entreated me to keep my politics to myself." He promised to come next day. "And pray see Champsenets," said Miss Elliot. "Nous verrons cela," he replied as he went out.

Champsenets, who had listened to the conversation from the next room, was terrified. The wretched man was certain that he would be denounced, arrested and executed that night. Every knock on the gate he thought was the arrival of the guards. When the servants had gone to bed, Mrs. Elliot went into his room and told him he must see the Duke himself the next day. After talking most of the night, he finally consented, saying that his life was in her hands.

The scene which followed is best told in her own words: "Champsenets then came into my room, and ten minutes later the Duke arrived. He started at seeing Champsenets, to whom he bowed and desired him to sit down. Poor Champsenets trembled so much that he could hardly stand. The Duke perceived this and turned to me and talked of my health. I was making tea, and when I had given the Duke his dish he turned to Champsenets and said, ' Cela ne vaut rien pour vous. You have been confined long and seem ill and weak: a bouillon would be better.'

"Champsenets then said, ' Monseigneur, you are all goodness. I have appeared very ungrateful to you. I wish to explain to your Highness why."

"The Duke replied very gravely, ' M. de Champsenets, no explanations. We will neither talk of the past nor on any other subject, but the situation of this good person who is trying to save your life at the expense of her own. She is ill, and I fear both you and her are in a scrape. I would be of use to you on her account if I could, but I fear that it is impossible. You and I must forget that we ever met before, as we never can again be in the same room; and I never wish to hear your name pronounced in my presence. My opinion of you has been fixed for some time. I am sorry that you cannot get away, as I shall not be at peace until I see you out of her house.' He then talked on different subjects—no politics of any kind."

Champsenets remained hidden in the house until the city barriers were opened, when Mrs. Elliot managed to get him to her house at Meudon, outside the walls. Philippe kept in constant communication and finally sent one of his old *valets de chambre* with a letter telling her that the mail cart which stopped at St. Denis would, for fifty louis, take Champsenets to Boulogne, where he could escape to England. At three o'clock in the morning they set off for St. Denis, when the mail cart came in an hour later and Mrs. Elliot, having paid the fifty louis, saw poor Champsenets "in a deplorable condition and much disguised, set off. There were other immigrants in the cart also. It was January, and quite dark."

Some years afterwards she heard that he had managed to get safely to England.

CHAPTER XXXI

ÉGALITÉ

O N September 15th the Commune of Paris issued the following decree:

" Upon the demand of Louis Philippe Joseph, Prince Français, the General Council decrees:

(1) Louis Philippe Joseph and his posterity will bear from henceforth as family name, Égalité.

(2) The garden known by the name of Palais Royal will be called henceforth, The Garden of the Revolution.

(3) Louis Philippe Joseph Égalité is authorised to mention the present decree in the execution of all legal documents."

Various interpretations have been given to this affair. Philippe was among the Paris candidates for election to the Convention. His change of name was said to be a gesture calculated to react favourably upon the electors. Danton in particular was backing him. It was one of the "crimes" for which Robespierre later sent him to the guillotine. Philippe himself was not at all sure of being elected. On September 19th he wrote to his son that there were only three more deputies to be nominated for Paris, and that he began to think that he would not be one of them. In that case he declared he would be delighted to join him again with the Army. There was no rancour in his forecast of defeat. His only comment was strangely ironical. "The Assembly," he added at the end of his letter, "will be excellent." He was elected the last of the Parisian deputies.

According to one of his fellow-deputies named Sergeant, the name of Égalité was due not to politics but to a bizarre sense of humour on the part of Manuel, the *procureur syndic* of the Paris commune. Philippe had gone to the Hôtel de Ville on September 15th to inquire about his own legal position and especially the legal position of his daughter, whom he feared would be classed among the *emigrés*. On the day before, he had addressed a letter to Manuel saying that he wanted the name of Orléans replaced by a name more in harmony with modern ideas, and during his visits the question naturally arose. There was nothing particularly strange about it, although the anti-Orléanists have made it into one more reason for sneering. But nobody thought it strange when the House of Hanover changed to the House of Windsor or Battenberg became Mountbatten. Why should they? It was conforming to overwhelming political circumstances. The name of Orléans signified the old régime —tyranny, aristocracy, privilege, everything, in fact, that was opposed to popular feeling at the moment. Philippe's wish for a name that would be free of these adjectives was natural enough if he intended to stay in France and follow the Revolution. But it was somewhat ridiculous for the first prince of the blood to jump to the other extreme and call himself Citizen Equality. According to Sergeant, when the question was being discussed, Manuel turned with a gesture to the statue of the nymph Equality, which adorned the municipal office, and said it would be an admirable name to adopt. Philippe shrugged his shoulders. "What could I say or do?" he said afterwards. "I had come to plead for my daughter, who was about to be declared an *emigrée*, and I had to sacrifice to that my repugnance at taking this burlesque name."

But whether he demanded it or accepted it, he had given himself an unenviable immortality.

CHAPTER XXXII

THE DECREE AGAINST THE EMIGRÉS

PHILIPPE took little or no part in the debates of the Convention. He had fled to the Mountain as an asylum where he could hide himself. He found it full of lunatics, who pointed at him and shouted his name. Under "Égalité," men persisted in seeing a Bourbon, and that name served to fan into flame all the fiercer hatred and fantastic suspicions without which no respectable revolution can be expected to exist for long. From the very beginning he became an object of mutual reproach, accusation and suspicion. Both sides of this furious assembly of men tossed him back and forth like a dud bomb that still might possibly go off.

The Right said, turning to the Left, "What is that Bourbon doing among the sansculottes? In raising him up on the Mountain, are you not trying to raise him higher still?" The Left, hurling itself solidly upon the Right, replied: "Yes, Égalité is on our side, but if there is anything of a Bourbon left in him it belongs to you." During all this clamour about him Philippe never breathed a word.

But outside the Convention we see him often, chiefly affected by the affairs of his children and his money; very grave, somewhat bewildered, and when he paused to reflect upon it, not a little astonished at

261

the strange society that surrounded him. It was said that in the interior apartments of the Palais Royal there was a royal suite maintained with all the splendour and ceremony of the old régime, where lackeys in full livery attended their lord with the formality and devotion of centuries, and where Philippe was no longer citoyen Égalité, but His Serene Highness and Monseigneur, Prince of the Blood, Duke of Orléans, etc. etc. The teller of this tale was a woman, who declared that she had found this strange scene when, on some businss or other, she had penetrated to the inner rooms. It is recounted by Ducoin, one of the innumerable anti-Orléanist writers. But whether it is true or the merest fancy, it is symbolic of something in Philippe's character during the last year of his life. Hidden away under the indifference, under the false title of Égalité, under the acquiescence in crime and corruption, there remained an inner apartment, furnished, not with any precious thoughts or remarkable desires, but with former customs and polite detachment. He once told Mrs. Elliot that he would willingly change his lot and all his fortune for a small estate and the life of an English country gentleman. And when she asked him why he did not get out of the hands of the vile people who surrounded him he said, "All this seems easy in your drawing-room. I wish that I could find it so easy; but I am in the torrent and must rise or fall with it."

During the autumn he had been intensely worried about his daughter's position in England. At the end of August he had written to Mme de Genlis ordering her return. He knew that a law condemning all *emigrés* to death who did not return by a certain date was being considered. In the hope of persuading the Convention to make an exception in cases of children who had gone abroad for their health or education, he prepared a memorandum setting forth the reasons for his daughter's sojourn in England.

Mme de Genlis received Philippe's letter with consternation. The idea of returning to Paris after the September massacres horrified her. She had had a very mixed reception in England, but anything seemed better than the dangers that awaited her in France. "They give me a very unpleasant account of Mme de Genlis, or de Sillery, or Brulard, as she is now called," wrote Fanny Burney. "They say she has established herself at Bury . . . with Mlle la Princesse d'Orléans and Pamela and a *Circe* (Henrietta de Cercey, her niece), another young girl under her care. . . . They form twenty, with themselves and household. They keep a botanist, a chemist and a natural historian always with them. These are supposed to have been common servants of the Duke of Orléans in former days, as they always walk behind the ladies when abroad; but, to make amends in the new equalising style, they all dine together at home. . . . They have been to a Bury ball, and danced all night, Mlle d'Orléans with anybody known or unknown to Madame Brulard."

"What a woeful change," sighed the shocked Miss Burney, "from that elegant, amiable, high-bred Madame de Genlis I knew six years ago! The apparent pattern of female perfection in manners, conversation and delicacy."

Yet in spite of the fact that she had shocked the respectable Miss Burney, been menaced by anonymous letters and denounced by the royalist *emigrés* as a Jacobin, Mme de Genlis and her two pupils, Mlle d'Orléans and Pamela, were finding life in England full of amusing adventures. Sheridan had taken them to Lacy House at Isleworth, where he gave balls and parties in their honour, and fell in love with Pamela, whom he declared to be the image of his dead wife.

Meanwhile, in Paris the law against the *emigrés* had been decreed, and on October 12th Mlle d'Orléans and Mme de Genlis had been inscribed on the fatal list. In desperation Philippe decided to prove that they were not *emigrés* by bringing them back and getting their names struck off. During the first week in November he sent Maret, the future Duke of Bassano, to London, with power of attorney to bring back Mlle d'Orléans. But it was not until the 20th that the party reached Calais, where, wrote Mme de Genlis, they were received "with great acclamations from a huge crowd—the last homage that the unhappy name of Orléans has received in France."

But Philippe had grown apprehensive. The travellers were met by a courier at Chantilly, where they stopped to change horses. There was a note from Philippe which read: "If you have not crossed the Channel, stay in England until further orders; if my courier finds you in France, stay in the place where you receive

this note and don't come to Paris. A second courier
will inform you what you must do."

"I did not pay any attention to this order," wrote
Mme de Genlis, "and I arrived that evening at Belle
Chasse. They were waiting for me, as I had sent on a
servant from Chantilly. At Belle Chasse I found M.
le duc d'Orléans, M. de Sillery, and five or six other
people." It was a sad meeting. Mlle d'Orléans was
weeping. Mme de Genlis, with the false dignity of a
pedant, made a little formal speech, handing over Mlle
to her father and giving her own resignation. She
had been offended that Maret should have been sent to
fetch her back. She knew that she was indispensable
at this moment and she took a calculated pleasure in
exploiting her advantage. Philippe was embarrassed
and dismayed. He led her into the next room and told
her that, because of the new decree, his daughter was
proscribed as an *émigrée* as she had not returned at
the stipulated date. He blamed her bitterly because she
had not brought her back when he had first written.
He said he was sure they would make an exception to
this new law but that meanwhile she would have to go
to a neutral country to await the outcome. It might
be for eight days. He would come and fetch his
daughter himself, but until then she must stay with
her and take care of her. She could not be so cruel as
to desert her now. Mme de Genlis says she replied
'coldly.' She would take Mlle to Tournay in Belgium
on condition that, if the decree of exception were not
passed within a fortnight, Philippe would send some
one to take her place."

The following day Philippe spoke in the Convention. His speech was a strange mixture of pleading, reasoning and caddishness. It lacked any force of personality, it had no sting in it.

The rulers of France must have felt very exalted as they considered whether the rigours of their outrageous law should be applied to a girl of fifteen whose feeble health had been the chief motive of sending her to take the waters at Bath. Philippe gave two further reasons for her absence—first, her education, and second, "to prevent her being influenced by the principles of a woman who no doubt was very estimable but whose opinions concerning present affairs have not always conformed to mine." This allusion to the Duchess of Orléans was singularly unfortunate. It could do nothing more than arouse the disdain of those who heard it, especially as any reference to a woman in public debate was considered bad form.

Although the Convention agreed to exempt children sent abroad for their education, the decree never came into force. Objections to individual cases made it necessary to frame a new law. Meanwhile the real power of the republic, the Commune, ordered Mlle Égalité, as she was now called, to leave Paris within twenty-four hours, and go and wait the decision of the Convention outside the territory of the Republic.

The day before the departure was spent at Belle Chasse, and Mme de Genlis has left a vivid picture of Philippe during that day. He was distracted, sombre, preoccupied. "There was something in his expression as though his mind were wandering—it was really sinister. He wandered from room to room, without stopping, as if he were afraid of conversation and of my questions. The weather was quite fair, so I sent Mlle, my niece and Pamela into the garden. When I was alone with the Duke of Orléans I began to talk to him about his situation. He hastened to interrupt me and replied brusquely that he had thrown in his lot with the Jacobins. I replied that after all that had happened, it was both a crime and a folly, that he would be their victim, and that already there was proof of it in this last decree which declared any French travellers above the age of fourteen to be *emigrés* who had not returned by last September. He must be blind not to see that the decree was aimed at him, by striking his daughter." Mme de Genlis begged him to take his family and go to America. Philippe, it appears, answered her by telling her that she knew nothing whatever of politics. "To change the conversation, as well as to satisfy my curiosity about something which astonished me very much," she wrote, "I asked him why he had left his coat-of-arms (three fleurs-de-lis) on the plaques above the fireplace, as these signs were proscribed by the decree. He replied, ' I have left them because it would have been cowardly to remove them' This reply," wrote Mme de Genlis, "was made in the curt tone that he used in any discussion but especially since the Revolution. The conversation," she said, "continued, and became very bitter and violent," when suddenly Philippe left her.

"We departed the next day; M. le Duc d'Orléans more sombre than ever gave me his arm to take me to the coach. I was very much disturbed. Mlle was in tears; her father was pale and trembling. When I was in the coach he stood motionless at the door, his eyes fixed on me. His look, full of sorrow and pain, seemed to implore pity. ' Adieu, Madame,' he said. The altered tone of his voice brought my agitation to a climax. Not able to say a single word, I held my hand out to him. He took it, grasped it strongly, then turning and walking quickly towards the postillions, he made a sign to them and we started."

CHAPTER XXXIII

POLITICAL FANFARE

SCARCELY had his daughter left for Tournay with Mme de Genlis and Pamela, than Philippe was once again drawn into the political whirlpool. On December 9th he published a letter in the *Moniteur*, denying that he had any ambitious designs on the liberty of the country either for himself or for his son. It seems extraordinary that such a manifesto should appear after the declaration of the Republic and still more extraordinary when, on December 6th, the Girondin Buzot demanded the exile of Philippe and his sons. "Let them carry elsewhere," he said, "the unhappiness of being clothed with a name that can serve as a rallying cry for factious persons or to emissaries of neighbouring powers, and with which the ear of a free man can no longer be wounded."

The adjournment was demanded when Louvet rose and delivered a pompous speech seconding Buzot's motion. Louvet was not blessed with a sense of humour. "Representatives of the people," he cried, "it is not I who wish to second the proposition of Buzot, it is the immortal founder of a famous republic, it is the father of Roman liberty—Brutus."

Murmuring broke out. But Louvet stuck to his guns.

"Yes, Brutus!" he shouted.

A member demanded a point of order. The President ruled that Louvet had the floor. And Louvet meant to keep it.

"Yes, Brutus . . . I am only his interpreter . . . Listen attentively to Brutus."

After this introduction, Brutus Louvet demanded "the exile of all the Bourbons, with the exception of the wife, the sister, and the children of Louis Capet, upon whose fate the Convention reserves judgment." This was opposed by Chabot, who declared that the judgment of the King should take place first. Chabot gave the interesting news that Robespierre and all his followers had opposed Philippe's election to the Convention.

St. Just followed by demanding the eternal exile of all the Bourbons and the death of any of them who should set foot again in France.

Merlin de Thionville burst out: "In 1788 I heard of an Orléanist faction—in 1789, '90 and '91 still an Orléanist faction. At present the name of Orléans is still a source of trouble in our midst. Let Orléans depart to-day. (Applause). But from the moment he departs, let the divisions, the discussions that torment us disappear forever and, true republicans, let us occupy ourselves in founding a government that can confound the first intriguer who wants to destroy liberty." (More applause).

But instead of bringing order into the debate this outburst, which was sensible enough in itself, only created more confusion. In spite of the fact that after Merlin's speech the discussion was declared to be closed,

Desmoulins rushed frantically to the tribune with the strange cry, "If this decree passes, France is lost!" An interesting diversion was now created by Barère, who was an intimate friend of Mme de Genlis. He suggested that the two ministers, Roland and Pasche, should be included in the decree against d'Orléans, and that the ministry should be reformed. Although the discussion had been closed already it was now closed a second time. But the tumult of voices continued. Finally the question concerning Philippe Égalité was adjourned for two days and a general decree was adopted, banishing members of the Bourbon Capet family who were in France except those in the Temple, within three days from Paris and within eight days from the territory of the Republic. This was mere prevarication. The decree had been aimed at Philippe. Barère put Philippe's case clearly when he had said, "I just begin to see the cause of the trouble. There is, it seems, a question of public right attached to this measure. This question is that one of the members of the branch of Bourbon Capet is in the position of being a representative of the people. . . . "

"That's it!" cried several voices.

In other words, could the Convention banish one of its own members? It was one of those questions of principle which offered a free field for a tournament of words and when, on the 15th, the question of Philippe Égalité was declared to be in the order of the day, the opponents and champions of Buzot's motion rushed into the fray with shouts of defiance. It is a strange scene to contemplate. After three years of revolution, a National Convention was occupying whole days in discussing a motion to exile one of their elected deputies because he belonged to a family called Bourbon Capet. In reality it was a fear and a belief that the royalist cause was still a live issue in the country.

Buzot, who had fathered the decree, opened the ball by saying that he did not care when the decree was adopted provided that after the trial of Louis XVI., "I don't see his successor behind the curtain."

A deputy named Faye spoke next, not, he said, by any means as a panegyrist of the Bourbons, nor as the intimate friend of Philippe Égalité, but to examine the position and to demand justice. There was only slight applause at this. Justice was not exactly the point in question. Faye's speech was oratorical but it was clear there were two aspects of the question. The first consisted in knowing whether the Convention could withdraw from one of its members the power which he had received from the sovereign people. The second consisted in knowing whether an individual, even if he came of a family of tyrants and traitors, should be banished from a society which had sworn equality and the abolition of despots. Having proved to his own satisfaction that the Convention could not banish its own members and that it certainly could not banish an individual without trial, Faye made a pretty rhetorical question and answered it himself. What crimes are imputed to Philippe Égalité? His birth. "Oh, Nature!" cried the orator, "Oh, Philosophy! what outrages are done to you! What! Crimes shall be hereditary! And you have said that virtues were not!"

At the end of the discussion, it was moved that the execution of the decree concerning the Bourbons should be suspended and the discussion adjourned until after the judgment of the King. Philippe, as usual, had not attended the meeting.

The most interesting light on this political fanfare is in the meetings of the Jacobin Club. Only here can the real motives be unveiled. On the evening of the 16th, the day Buzot had first proposed his decree of banishment, Desmoulins informed the club that the Convention had had the most tumultuous session which had ever occurred since the beginning of the Revolution. Buzot's decree was, he said, aimed at banishing Égalité, "who had contributed so much to the Revolution. To demand the banishment of this sincere friend of liberty, is to demand that he be assassinated at Coblenz (the concentration point of the royalist émigrés). That was the design of the Brissotins. They said to themselves, "The patriots will not want to abandon Égalité, and we will make the Mountain appear to be a faction. We were very embarrassed. We think it very unpolitic to exile the son of Égalité as well as their brother-in-arms, Valence, a nephew of Sillery, who would accompany them into exile—it is a means of disorganising the army. We were very embarrassed. Merlin's impolitic motion on the subject of royalty had made our conduct difficult—it was the height of art to make us pass for royalists in forcing us to defend Égalité. You can judge what joy it was for the prisoners in the Temple (the Royal Family) to learn that they wanted to exile Égalité."

"The aim of the Brissotins," continued Desmoulins, "is to put us in the position either of being unjust or of being royalists. They want to make themselves popular by exaggerating republican principles, and they want to force Égalité to appeal to the people, and once having done that, they can use the same methods to exclude other deputies by the same means. They can even get an appeal to the people for Louis XVI. and save him. Such are the true tactics of the Brissotins (or Girondists, as they are more generally known)."

Robespierre followed Desmoulins. His speech is particularly interesting as he had not been at the sessions of the Convention. Moreover, in a few months time, it was he who would send both Desmoulins and Philippe to the guillotine. He adopted his usual cautious and pedantic methods. His aim was to destroy the Girondists and the Orléanists by making them destroy each other. He walked with delicate steps among prospective corpses. He was neat and perfumed in an atmosphere of blood. He was neither Girondist nor Jacobin nor Orléanist. He disentangled himself from all the threads and emerged a Robespierrist. "The patriots," he explained, "that is to say the Jacobins, had appeared to defend the citizen Égalité because they thought the cause of principles was attached to the cause of Égalité. One thing is certain —the patriots have never had contact with the House of Orléans, and those who provoked this decree have the greatest possible contact with the House. How does it happen that d'Orléans was nominated deputy to the Convention by those who were in touch with Brissot? How does it happen that Louvet has spread the rumour that we want to raise d'Orléans to the throne? How does it happen that Louvet, who knows very well that I voted against Égalité in the electorial Assembly, has spread his libels that I want to give the crown to d'Orléans?"

One has a sudden glimpse of how small the Revolution had become, how personal, how controlled from one point. Twenty-five million people were being affected (more than the combined number of people in England and America) incalculable changes which would affect the whole European system were occurring, and yet such rhetorical accusations were valid, potent and terrible in their results. Robespierre was a master of making the personal allusion convey a sinister menace even to the point of ridicule. [1]

"As for me," continued Robespierre, "for a long time I have had the project of demanding the exile of all the Bourbons, and the demand is not in the least inhuman, as has been said, for they can take refuge in London and the nation can provide in an honourable manner for the subsistence of the exiled family. They have not deserved ill of the country; their exclusion is not at all a punishment but a measure of safety, and if the members of their family love true principles,

[1] For example, one of the accusations which sent Danton to the guillotine was that he had attended parties at the house of a certain Robert, where Orléans had mixed the punch.

they will feel honoured with this exile, because it is always honourable to serve the cause of liberty.

"I therefore invite my colleagues to vote for the decree presented by Buzot; and I invite them at the same time to oppose the consequences which the Brissotins want to produce against the best friends of the people."

This equivocation did not please Marat at all. He rushed to the tribune and cried, "Robespierre seems to raise doubts about the project of the Brissotin faction —at the same time he is not opposed to the exile of Égalité. I am far from approving of Robespierre. Égalité must remain (loud applause from the Assembly and the galleries) because he is the representative of the people. To-day the criminal faction who want to attack the rights of the people in the person of Égalité would like to exile all the friends of the people, and you yourself, Robespierre, you will be at their head. Let Égalité remain among us." Marat was furiously applauded.

On the 19th, when the decree had been suspended until after the King's trial, there was some further discussion at the club, but Philippe had now become a mere political football between Jacobin and Girondist. Those who belonged to neither party looked on with amazement.

"How," wrote the journalist Prudhomme, intending to be devastating, "how could Philippe Égalité be dangerous? How could the French love a man who only seems to have loved the English; who liked to be

among them more than among us; who has only
English people around him?"

To close the affair, Marat issued a profession of
faith. He declared that he had opposed the decree of
Buzot because he considered that the Convention did
not have the right to deprive a citizen of his quality of
deputy and could not do so without attacking the
national sovereignty and usurping absolute power,
thus making it independent of the nation itself. Put
into other terms, Marat was afraid that the extreme
Jacobin minority, including himself, could be gradually
excluded by this method. Therefore he supported
Philippe's parliamentary rights. As for Philippe as a
man, Marat wrote that "he was an unworthy favourite
of fortune without virtue, soul or guts, whose only
merit was the gibberish of debauch." It would appear
from this and other equally picturesque epithets that
Marat did not receive the fifteen thousand francs that
he had asked for. He concluded his profession by
declaring that if the nation ever had to choose a chief
as he considered it would inevitably be obliged to do,
d'Orléans would be the last man upon whom he would
cast his eyes—in fact he would suffer martyrdom
rather than give him his vote.

After all this fog of rhetoric and accusation it is
almost a shock to find Philippe, on December 26th, in
his seat among the Parisian deputies of the Mountain,
when Louis XVI. appeared at the bar of the Convention to present his defence against the charges
which had been made against him. In the long and
stormy debate which followed, certain deputies de-

manded immediate judgment. Others attempted to delay such sudden action. Royalty, said Pétion, had been abolished by an act of the Convention. Louis Capet, therefore, was King no longer. Thus the question resolved itself into a pronouncement upon the fate of an individual. "We have all sworn," he cried, "that we will not have a King! Who is there who will go back on his oath? Who wants a King? No! we do not want one!"

At this the whole Convention, according to the official report, leapt to its feet. Philippe Égalité and several other members were particularly noticeable, waving their hats violently as a sign of adherence to Pétion's words.

On December 9th he had published his denial of Kingly ambitions.

On December 26th, he waved his hat for no more Kings.

On January 16th, he would vote for the death of the dethroned King Louis XVI.

CHAPTER XXXIV

REGICIDE

AT about seven-thirty on the evening of January 16th, a little group of Philippe's friends gathered at Hotel St. Marc in the rue St. Marc, where Biron was living. There was a feeling of strained anxiety in the room as each person arrived. The others inquired anxiously if there was any further news of the King's trial. Biron, now a General, had come to Paris some days before to clear himself of a denunciation that had been made against him by a bloodthirsty Jacobin named Rossignol. He had seen Philippe at Grace Elliot's house, where the talk had been entirely about the King's trial which was then proceeding to its climax. "I hope, Monseigneur," Mrs. Elliot had said, "that you will vote for the King's deliverance."

"Certainly," said Philippe sarcastically, "and for my own death."

Biron had interrupted and said that Philippe would pretend illness on the day of the voting and stay away.

Mrs. Elliot goes so far as to say that Philippe told her himself that this was what he intended to do.

Yet whatever his intentions may have been in Mrs. Elliot's drawing-room, Philippe had been present in the Convention on Tuesday, January 11th. The trial had resolved itself into three questions.

1.—Is Louis Capet guilty of conspiracy against

public liberty and of attempts against the general security of the country? Philippe Égalité had voted— yes. The minutes record that there was a movement of indignation in the hall as he gave his vote.

2.—Shall the judgment be referred to the sanction of the people? Philippe Égalité had said, "I am only concerned with my duty. I say no."

On Wednesday, January 16th, there remained the third question. What punishment has Louis, former King of France, merited?

During the day Mrs. Elliot had received a note from Biron asking her to come to the hotel and saying that he had arranged to have lists of the votes brought in every half-hour. She arrived about half-past seven and found every one very dismal. The voting in the convention hall was to begin at eight o'clock. Almost exactly at that hour news was brought that Philippe had that moment entered the Convention and taken his seat. The lists began to arrive, each other more ominous than the last. Finally the consternation of the little party reached its height when the list of the Parisian deputies arrived, containing Philippe's vote for death. Mrs. Elliot was horror-struck and burst into tears. Biron was almost in a fit. A young *aide-de-camp* of Philippe's tore off his coat and flung it in the fire, saying he would blush ever to wear it again.

Away in London, when the Prince of Wales heard the news, he snatched the Reynold's portrait of Philippe from the wall at Carlton House and tore it to pieces.

Philippe had voted last of the Parisian deputies. According to the account of one who was there a feeling of lassitude had crept over the galleries. Hour after hour the deputies followed each other to the tribune uttering the words death, imprisonment or banishment. Some of them explained their votes; most of them did not. Philippe Égalité was called. At this name silence became more general and even the knitters interrupted their work for a moment. Philippe slowly mounted the steps of the tribune and said:

"Solely influenced by a sense of duty, convinced that all those who have attacked or will attack the sovereignty of the people deserve death, I vote for death."

For a moment there was a tense silence of stupefaction and disgust, then suddenly all the people in the galleries who had come to ask for the head of Louis XVI. broke out in insults, boos and hisses as Philippe Égalité resumed his seat in the Assembly.

. . . .

Mrs. Elliot saw him once again, about six weeks after the King's death. She had been taken ill. When Philippe heard of it he had sent an old and faithful *valet de chambre* with an affectionate letter, saying that he did not dare to come to see her but begging her to see him when she was well again, "saying that all the world had given him up and that he thought his unhappy lot would have made me forgive him if I thought he had done wrong." Philippe is generally best interpreted through women and his meeting with Mrs. Elliot after he had become a regicide gives some indication of his state of mind. She was much agitated at the idea of seeing him. Philippe came in dressed in deep mourning. He looked embarrassed and very grave. Mrs. Elliot asked him if his black coat was for the King. Philippe forced a smile and said, "Oh, no. I am in mourning for my father-in-law, the Duc de Penthièvre."

"I suppose," said Mrs. Elliot, "that the King's death has hastened his: or perhaps the manner of his cruel trial and your having voted for death." She burst into tears. "I dare say he died broken-hearted; and so shall I. But you, Monseigneur, will die like the poor King—on the scaffold."

"Good God!" cried Philippe, "what a state you are in! . . . The King has been tried and he is no more. I could not prevent his death."

"But you promised you would not vote."

Philippe got up. "This is an unpleasant subject. You cannot, must not judge for me. I know my own situation. I could not avoid doing what I have done. I am perhaps more to be pitied than you can form an idea of. I am more a slave of faction than any one in France . . . Things are at their worst. I wish you were in England. If money can procure you a passport I will give you five hundred pounds. That is my last resource for you. The rulers like money and I have some hopes for you."

As she was leaving, Philippe told her that people said she had been very imprudent in her professions of royalism. "If you like to wear mourning for the King, for God's sake wear it," he exclaimed, "but say it is for some of your relations, or you will get into a scrape and I shall never be able to get you out of it. I wish that you could have remained in the country until you obtained a passport for England. I wish that *I* had never left it, but now I can never see it again."

If the exact words of this conversation were partially invented or incorrectly recalled years afterwards the general tone of the interview stands out clearly. Philippe's gravity, the brusque manner which Mme de Genlis also remarked that he had developed since the Revolution, the feeling of being shut in and hunted by unseen but implacable forces, and with it all a certain air of *hauteur*, nonchalance, indifference.

After this interview Grace Elliot disappears from Philippe's life. She did not obtain a passport. She was arrested and spent eighteen months in the revolutionary prisons, after which she returned to England and was once more received into royal favour by the Prince of Wales.

She often returned to Paris during the restoration and the Empire. "Her daughter, Lady Charles Bentick, used to say that on looking around on the brilliant assemblage of lovely women to be found in the Opera House in London, she saw no one comparable to her mother for beauty and elegance of manner." She died on May 15th, 1823.

After these personal accounts of this famous episode, certain questions remain. Why, in the first place, did Philippe not emigrate before the trial when he had been given the chance by Robespierre and others to go into exile in England? He attempted to answer this himself by saying that his present circumstances were exactly similar to those after the October days in

1789, when Lafayette had exiled him to London. "The same means, the same forms are employed," he wrote, "to persuade me to absent myself. I find all the same things except the dull, cold face of Lafayette. I have sworn to maintain liberty and equality with all my power or to die at my post."

But there were other reasons. The question of his property and his fortune demanded his presence in Paris. The previous summer he had come to an understanding with his creditors, if we are to believe a letter written to his sons on July 20th. By this arrangement he said that he expected to have at the beginning of 1793, one million seven hundred thousand livres income, "without owing anything to any one, and with hopes of an increase." This was very much less than his income had been before, but it was still a large sum. Some of the capital was undoubtedly in England, but a large part of it still remained in France and could only be protected by his presence. Lands, houses, shops and personal treasures would have been confiscated immediately had he emigrated. He had thrown in his lot with the popular party. By this means he hoped to secure his own safety and the safety of his children. He might as well have trusted himself to the mercy of wild buffaloes.

Why did he vote for the King's death? Ambition, hate, revenge, fear—all have been given as reasons, and each one enters somewhat into the decision. But the ambition was not to become king but to become free of the power that had frustrated him at every turn in his life. The Court had been to him like some duty-bound, restraining father to an impetuous and stubborn boy. Yet even so, he did not need to condemn his cousin to death. He could have abstained from voting and still have been a good patriot. He did not think so. He expected to flatter the popular party. He hoped to make sure of the future for himself and for his children. He knew that the motion for his exile had only been postponed. He voted for his own future.

CHAPTER XXXV

ARREST

ON March 26th Robespierre again brought up the question of exiling the remaining Bourbons. He made one exception. He demanded immediate judgment upon Marie Antoinette. But the Convention refused to discuss either of the motions and passed to the order of the day. There appeared to be a lull in the storm of fear that surrounded the name of Bourbon. Not for long, however. On April 1st, the Convention listened to a report of three commissioners who had been sent to investigate conditions at the front in Belgium, where Dumouriez had been forced to fall back after the battle of Nerwinden. The commissioners had reached Tournay and had met the General in the house of Madame de Genlis. Mlle Égalité and Pamela were also present and the General Égalité (the Duc de Chartres) and General Valence were in attendance upon Dumouriez. In fact it was quite a family party. Dumouriez had spoken in violent terms of the Convention and the Jacobins. "They were," he shouted, "all regicides and tyrants." He laughed at their decrees and swore that he would not tolerate the revolutionary tribunal. The delegates of the Convention remonstrated. Instead of altering his tone, Dumouriez became more violent in his language. He declared he would march on Paris, shut up the Jacobin Club and dissolve the Convention. He would re-establish the former constitution, bad though it was, and he would put a king on the throne. He was emphatic that there must be a king, whoever it was.

During this tirade the commissioners said that Mme de Genlis had smiled "malignantly."

The effect on the Convention was terrifying, and the debates, if they can be dignified by the word, between April 1st and April 12th, read like the wrangling of demented savages. Lasource immediately demanded the arrest of the citizens Égalité and Sillery, and the following day the *Moniteur* announced that orders of arrest had been made out to include Pamela, who had recently married Lord Edward Fitzgerald and had gone to Ireland. Laclos, [1] Lemaire, one of Philippe's treasurers and Philippe's two sons, Montpensier and Beaujolais, aged seventeen and twelve, were also arrested.

A few days later Marat demanded a price on the head of the Duc de Chartres, but the future King of the French, though he followed Dumouriez into the Austrian lines, disdained to fight against his country and escaped to Switzerland, where he was an object of hatred to the Royalists and of suspicion to the Revolutionists.

For Philippe all this had most serious consequences.

---

[1] Laclos, "that damned soul of the House of Orléans" was imprisoned in the Abbaye. The taint of Orléanism lay thickly around him, yet this master of intrigue always seemed to have another trick up his sleeve. How he escaped what appeared to be certain death will never be exactly known. Yet escape he did, and lived to be a General of Artillery under Napoleon. His learned biographer, M. Dard, claims that certain discoveries of Laclos were responsible for the development of modern artillery. He died of dysentery in Sept., 1803, at Tarento, carrying into silence more intriguing memories than most men collect during their lives.

A letter from Chartres had been stopped by the censor and was read in the Convention. It was dated March 30th, from Tournay. "My rose colour," wrote the young General, "is at the moment quite past and it has changed into the most profound black. I see liberty lost. I see the National Convention completely ruining France by forgetting all principles. I see civil war kindled. I see innumerable armies descending from all sides upon our unhappy country, and I do not see the army to oppose them. Our line regiments are almost destroyed, the strongest battalions have only four hundred men . . . the volunteers desert and fly in all directions . . . they cannot be stopped, and the Convention believes that with these troops it can wage war against all Europe. I assure you that for the little while this will last they will be disillusioned. Into what abyss are they hurling France?"

Such was the temper of men's minds, that this letter would have been enough to condemn its writer to the guillotine, had he surrendered himself to the mercy of the Convention.

Philippe refused to believe that his son was a traitor. When he first heard the news he sent off a hurried note by a courier to Tournay. "An officer of the General Staff," he wrote, "told me something about you yesterday that I cannot believe. Is it possible that you have been so blinded? No, I cannot believe it. I will see you arrive at the bar of the Convention and prove your innocence. Should it be otherwise I will be the most unhappy of fathers." But Chartres was already beyond the claws of the Convention, and even

PAMELA

if he received this note he had no intention of putting his head under the knife in defence of his innocence.

The session of April 4th in the Convention was incredibly wild. Mob hysteria and mob vengeance seemed to have reached a climax. "For five months," cried Barbaroux, "we have denounced the Orléans faction and for five months we have been treated as scoundrels. To-day you recognise that we are right. What in fact does Dumouriez demand? The re-establishment of the old constitution. Who is it that the old constitution calls to the throne? It is Orléans." There were loud murmurs, which broke into cheers as another deputy demanded that Sillery and Orléans be put under guard. It is noteworthy that Philippe was always called d'Orléans and not Égalité during these explosions. Men could not get away from the shadow of monarchy. They still hovered about it in fascination. They made an idol out of their fears and sacrificed a nation to it.

When this first demand for detention had been made Sillery and Philippe both did a brave thing. They welcomed the order to keep them under guard and demanded that their papers should be examined. Both of them declared that if it were proved that Valence, who was Sillery's son-in-law, and Chartres were guilty of treason they, the respective fathers, would be the first to demand justice upon their sons.

Two days later, on April 6th, when it was definitely announced that Dumouriez, Valence and Chartres had gone over to the enemy, Carrier, the future terrorist of Nantes, demanded that Philippe and Sillery be immediately arrested as accomplices to the treason.

Now a curious thing happened. Marat replied to Carrier. He said there was no convincing proof whatever against either Égalité or Sillery, and he demanded that, instead of being arrested, they should consider themselves in a state of detention in order to establish their innocence.

But this moderation of Marat was intolerable to a Convention that was determined to find victims—and coming from Marat, it was doubly suspect. An eloquent deputy named Fonfredi cried: "Let all the Bourbons be arrested and held as hostages, and if the princes who are all of a kind dare to bring an assassin's knife against us, let the Bourbon heads fall on the scaffold." This proposition was adopted unanimously.

The Convention was now in full cry. Lacroix shouted that the women and children of the House of Orléans should be arrested at once. This was bravely adopted, and the Duchess of Orléans (citoyen Égalité), Mme de Valence and her children, and Mme de Montesson, the second wife of Philippe's father, were included in the orders for arrest.

While the Convention was busy about the wording of the decree, Philippe was dining at the Palais Royal with a friend named de Moinville. The fish course was being served when a deputy, Merlin de Douai, came in and told Philippe that the Convention was determined to destroy him.

"Great God!" exclaimed Philippe, putting his hand to his forehead, "is it possible? After all the proofs of patriotism, after all the sacrifices, to strike me with a decree like that. What ingratitude! The horror of it! What do you think of it, Moinville?"

Moinville was slowly squeezing the juice of a lemon on to a fillet of sole in front of him.

"Frightful, Monseigneur," he said, "but what do you expect—they have got all that they could from Your Highness? You are no more use to them, and they are doing with Your Highness what I will do with this lemon when I have squeezed all the juice out of it."

As he spoke, de Moinville threw the two halves of the lemon into the fireplace, and, observing to Philippe that sole should be eaten while it was really hot, he continued his meal.

Philippe was arrested in his bed in the Palais Royal at four o'clock the following morning.

CHAPTER XXXVI

IMPRISONMENT

LATER in the morning of April 7th, he was conducted to the Mayor's office in the Hôtel de Ville, where the decree ordering the arrest of the Bourbons was shown to him. He immediately addressed a note to the president of the Convention demanding a suspension of the decree in his case until his conduct could be examined and his innocence established. He justified his demand by his position as a representative of the people. The suspension was refused and a deputy named Perrières made the curious suggestion that Philippe should reassume the name of d'Orléans or Bourbon and not be allowed to bear the name Égalité any more than any other citizen. No one seconded this motion. Indeed it needed no seconding, for Philippe had never lost the name of Bourbon d'Orléans in spite of all the nymphs of equality in Paris. At about eight o'clock in the evening of April 7th, he was taken from the Hôtel de Ville to the prison of l'Abbaye, where his youngest son, Beaujolais was already locked up.

This was only a temporary imprisonment, for the Convention, fearing to have the Bourbons in Paris even though they were in prison, ordered them to be transferred to Marseilles under a strong guard.

Not until April 11th did the journey begin. The

papers announced briefly that "Philippe Égalité and his third son, as well as the citizens Bourbon, his sister, and the ci-devant Prince de Conti have left Paris to report at Marseilles, conforming to the decree of the Convention. The citoyen Égalité (the Duchess of Orléans) is still sick and could not accompany them."

The journey was a weary one, the post horses were few and far between, the lodgings shabby and vermin-ridden, the food bad and expensive, besides which a detachment of gendarmes accompanying them took every possible occasion of airing their views about aristocrats. The old Prince de Conti spent the time complaining of everything in a loud voice; the Duchesse de Bourbon began the journey in a very bad temper. At one moment she was so angry at the commissioners appointed by the Convention to accompany the prisoners that she completely lost the use of her voice. But later she became more reasonable. "We offered her the services of a doctor," reported the commissioners, "but she replied that she only needed to rest. She asked us permission to hear Mass to-morrow, Sunday. We consented and we will take all necessary pre-cautions to prevent the occurrence of any dangerous incident." As the little party of travellers continued the journey the weather became so bad that their progress was reduced to a few miles a day. In the villages crowds of inquisitive peasants and artisans flocked around the slow-moving carriages, staring at the travellers with impudent and hostile looks: "A prodigious affluence of curious people," reads the report, "who, moved by perfidious men, could have made our position very difficult."

During these harrowing and uncertain days the little Comte de Beaujolais slept, and Philippe whistled the time away in cheerful indifference to the bad weather, the dirty inns or the stares of the villagers. Sometimes the crowds were moved by something more than curiosity as the *cortège* arrived at the village inn. At Orgon, for example, the inhabitants "were moved by an excess of patriotism and wine " to offer their voluntary services in conducting the prisoners to their destination. Not until after midnight could they be persuaded to retire firing off their guns and crying: " *Tous les Bourbons à la Guillotine.*" At Aix they were met by a huge crowd and had to be protected by an armed guard supplied by the municipality. They were shut up in one room of the town hall, where they were all obliged to sleep together. The commisioners did not dare to suggest anything else; the menaces of the crowd had been too frightful.

Precautions against mob violence of the most loathsome kind had become absolutely essential. News of the arrival of the Bourbons had spread rapidly in Marseilles, and the streets and squares buzzed with excitement. It was, said the people, like Capet himself returning from Varennes or on his way to the guillotine. To prevent the Marseillais from taking the law into their own bloodthirsty hands, the prisoners were brought into the city at four o'clock in the morning of April 23rd, and taken immediately to the fort of Notre Dame de la Garde. The Duchesse de

Bourbon was so exhausted by the hardships and terrors of the journey that she had to be carried into the fort in a chair. Nothing was prepared to receive the prisoners but bare rooms with straw on the stone floors. At the sight of these miserable quarters the poor lady broke down, complaining bitterly at the barbarous treatment.

Once inside the fort, the commissioners sighed with relief as they handed over their charges to the local authorities. They had been as considerate as it was possible to be under the most difficult circumstances, and it is a welcome relief in the middle of the Terror to read the conclusion of their report to the Convention. "Our mission is ended," they wrote, "we have paid our tribute to the fatherland, but at this moment, given over entirely to feelings of humanity which are inseparable from true patriotism, we cannot help confessing that the situation of this unhappy lady (the Duchesse de Bourbon) has wrung our souls and we are not afraid to proclaim it aloud. The citizen Conti, because of his age and his infirmities, is not less to be pitied, and feels the bitterness of his position very deeply. As for citizen Égalité he shows more resolution than the others and appears to find in the company of his children weapons against the boredom and the sadness of his solitude. His son Antoine (the duc de Montpensier) had been brought to this fort two hours before.

．　　．　　．　　．　　．　　．　　．

While Philippe had been journeying across France to Marseilles the Convention had fought over his

name in paroxysms of rage and denunciation. Girondists and Jacobins hurled accusations of Orléanism at
each other and retorted with furious denials. Nothing
is deader than dead politics, yet during these death
grapples over the name of Orléans you can feel the
desperate spirit of revolution choking itself with blood.
Page after page resounds with passionate assertion and
counter assertion. On April 12th, to take only one
example, Petion, accused by the Mountain of Orléanism
was like a man with his back to the wall armed with a
rapier against a pack of wolves. Interrupted by
Marat he cried, "I am honoured by calumnies from
Marat, he only vilifies those whom he praises."
Accused of being the accomplice of Orléans, he
retorted: "When it came to the question of expelling
the Bourbons I gave him some advice which perhaps
could have saved the country. He did not take the
advice."

"Pétion," cried the painter David, "were you in
correspondence with *Égalité fils*?"

"Yes, yes, yes, a hundred times yes—and it would
have been better if he hadn't had any with other people
—he wouldn't be a traitor to-day and he would be far
from France." Petion's voice rose in a crescendo of
impotent fury. "*I* conspire against the republic—
I conspire for Orléans—*I* who wanted him to resign
from the Convention!" Petion's voice continued and
was lost in the cry of the Jacobin pack. It was only a
few months before he would be found dead, half-eaten
by dogs in a field in the Gironde.

On April 16th the confiscation of the Orléans

property was demanded and decreed. Agents were sent to the Palais Royal to make inventories of Philippe's personal effects, all of which were to be sold at auction. There were some curious discoveries. The agents found that Philippe had a collector's passion. There was a large collection of shoe-buckles "valuable enough to make the fortune of a jeweller." There were walking-sticks of every kind and shape arranged neatly in racks; there were collections of pipes and a great number of portfolios laid away in drawers. Everything indicated a character that loved order and was careful about details.

All loans made in the name of Orléans had been declared to be national, and three deputies, Cambercérès, Mathieu and Ruhl, were ordered to search his personal papers and to report upon what they found. On June 21st they declared to the Convention that they had found nothing whatever among the papers to indicate that Philippe had ever made any attempt upon the throne. But they found many other things which doubtless they considered it was best to say nothing about. For many of the members of the Convention, who were at that moment wildly denouncing Orléanism, were in fact under obligation to Philippe. There were receipts for money and letters filled with the most flattering proposals. All this evidence is now unfortunately lost, and it is impossible to untangle the parliamentary corruption that was hidden underneath the activities of Girondist and Jacobin. When in 1810 Savary, the Duke de Rovigo, replaced Fouché as Napoleon's minister of police, he read through the

entire lot of Orléans papers and took a selection of them
to the Emperor at Rambouillet. After examining them
with the greatest attention, Savary declares that
Napoleon said:

"You see how little we should trust to appearances.
You had a prejudice against this prince, and if you
had found an opportunity of injuring any one of his
party you would have been carried away by the feelings
of resentment which had perhaps been instilled into
your mind by those very persons who were under
obligation to him. This proves to me that the Duke of
Orléans was not a bad man. If he had had the vices
which have tainted his memory, nothing could have
stopped him from carrying out the project he was
supposed to have had. He was nothing more than a
lever in the hands of the agitators of the period. . . .

"I feel no interest in the matter. I believe that an
Orléanist party has existed during the period of our
internal discords. I even think it might be revived
were the throne to become vacant, but so long as I
live it is a chimerical idea which will never win any
proselytes.

"Burn all this trash and don't molest any of the
people mentioned nor let them know that I have read
those papers. It would embarrass them."

CHAPTER XXXVII

THE LAST JOURNEY

THE young duc de Montpensier has left a vivid and sensitive account of his imprisonment at Marseilles. He had been brought to the fort of Notre Dame de la Garde only a few hours before the arrival of the other members of his family. After the local authorities had assigned them their miserable rooms Montpensier was allowed to join his father and his younger brother Beaujolais, who had been put together in one room. He was impressed at once by his father's cheerfulness and equanimity. "At least," said Philippe, "we can be happy that they haven't separated us." In fact the conditions of their imprisonment were bearable for the first few days. Beds, tables and chairs were put into the rooms, and although the old Prince de Conti might complain and the Duchess resign herself to God, Philippe and his two boys enjoyed each other's company, dined and supped together, read books and discussed their chances for an early release. As there was no charge against them whatever, except the fact that they were Bourbons, they had every reason to believe that this was possible. But about four days later they received a rude shock to their hopes. Three local administrators suddenly appeared while they were having lunch. The room was scarcely big enough to hold them, but they crowded in and announced

that henceforth the members of the Bourbon family
would not be allowed to communicate with each
other. Philippe at once protested and demanded to
know whence this order had come. The officials
replied that they did not know for certain, but it had
probably been decreed by the Convention. Montpensier
burst out with all the impetuosity of his eighteen
years: "Your law is barbarous and tyrannic. It
would be better to shoot us or guillotine us on the
spot than to let us die like this by slow fire." His
father urged him to keep calm as he was led away.
Yet even now the decree of separation was not rigidly
observed, and occasionally the three prisoners were
allowed to have a meal together.

A week later Philippe was questioned before a local
tribunal, which appears to have shown him an unusual
amount of respect. Nothing whatever was found in
his replies to implicate him with Dumouriez or to
show that he had had designs on the throne. But in
spite of this he was led back to prison to await the
decision of the higher authority at Paris.

Towards the 22nd or 23rd of May he was taken
alone and heavily guarded by troops and gendarmes
to the fort of St. Jean, where he was locked up in
solitary confinement in one of the gloomy towers.
Eight days later the other prisoners were transferred
to the same prison and Beaujolais was consigned once
more to the same room with his father. In this
horrible prison they passed the next five months.
Montpensier was confined in a lower room of the same
tower so dark, so stinking and so horrible that he

could only exclaim "Quoi! c'est ici?" when he was thrust through the iron doorway. Philippe addressed several vain appeals to be allowed a little fresh air and exercise for himself and his boys. Pompous officials, enormously impressed with their own authority, appeared at the door of his cell and informed him solemnly that it was impossible. Philippe was cheerful and not in the least impressed. He pointed out that Beaujolais, who was only thirteen, was suffering from his imprisonment and his health was declining. His persistence finally obtained permission for the child to go out in the prison yard for an hour each day accompanied by a jailor.

Sometimes they had a guard who was more human than the others, and allowed Montpensier to go up the tower stairs and spend an hour or two with his father and brother while he kept watch below lest some officer or local administrator should appear out of curiosity to stare at the illustrious prisoners. These fugitive meetings are described with a pathetic joy, and Montpensier always returned to his dungeon strengthened by his father's good humour.

On October 15th Philippe heard that he was to be taken to Paris. Beaujolais had heard the news during his outing, and came in with a white, scared face. Philippe asked him what the matter was. "There is something about you in the papers," said Beaujolais." "If that's all," said Philippe, "it is nothing new. They do me that honour often enough; but I should like to read that paper very much if you can get it for me." "I saw it in my aunt's room, and she didn't want me to say anything to you about it; but I thought you would rather know." "You are quite right," replied Philippe. "But tell me, is it at the Convention that there has been some question about me?" "Yes, Papa," said Beaujolais. "It has been decided that you will be put on trial." "So much the better!" exclaimed Philippe. "This must all finish soon, one way or the other. And what have they to accuse me of? Embrassez-moi, mes enfants, je suis enchanté!"

"I was far from sharing in his delight," wrote Montpensier, recalling this scene, "but at the same time his perfect sense of security, and the tendency one always has to flatter oneself with what one desires, prevented me from feeling as anxious as I would have felt had I learned the fatal news in his absence."

Philippe was allowed to see the paper. When he had read the decree of accusation against him he exclaimed, "It is not based on anything whatever; it has been applied for by a lot of rogues. But it doesn't matter; I defy them to find anything against me!"

His optimism seemed to be justified when three commissioners arrived from Paris to arrange for his journey. They were extremely polite, and explained that it was less a matter of a trial than an explanation, a clearing up of certain matters, that was wanted. Like so many hundreds of other victims of the savage tribunal who could not believe that the vague generalities of the decrees could thrust them into death,

Philippe set out for Paris on October 23rd in a calm and optimistic state of mind.

At five o'clock in the morning he woke up Montpensier to bid him farewell. "I wanted to go without saying it," he said, embracing him; "but I couldn't resist this desire to see you once more before going. Adieu, my child. Console yourself, console your brother, and think both of you of the happiness we all will have when we meet again."

"Alas!" wrote Montpensier, "that happiness was not destined for us. Unhappy and excellent father! Whoever saw you intimately and knew you well will be forced to agree (unless he is a worthless calumniator) that you had neither ambition nor desire for vengeance in your heart; that you possessed the most amiable and solid qualities; but that perhaps you lacked that firmness which leads one to act only according to one's own will; that besides you gave your confidence too easily and that unscrupulous men found means of abusing it to ruin you and sacrifice you to their atrocious schemes."[1]

On his journey to Paris Philippe was accompanied by a faithful servant named Gamasche, who had refused to leave his master and had served him in his miserable dungeon. He belonged to a family which had long been devoted to the House of Orléans, and his account of Philippe's last journey is a precious document which has given poor Gamasche a celebrity

[1] After 43 months in prison the two boys were released on condition that they left the country. They embarked for America, where their elder brother had gone into voluntary exile. Later, Montpensier and Beaujolais lived at Twickenham, near London. They died in 1807, within a few days of each other, as a result of the hardhips they had suffered in prison.

which he certainly was far from imagining. He knew and cared nothing about politics, but he loved his master, and he tells his brief story with a charming sincerity.

He said that Philippe seemed pleased that his imprisonment had ended. "Monseigneur left fort Saint Jean on October 23rd, after having embraced his two sons. One cannot recall this separation without the most painful feelings, as these illustrious captives never saw each other again.

"The coach was escorted by gendarmes. When the Prince arrived at Aix he asked the commissioners if it was possible to send their troop away, as he thought he was perfectly safe among them, and he was not in the least disturbed. The commissioners were very flattered by what the Prince had told them, and answered him that they would avoid anything that might displease him. The gendarmes were dismissed. The Prince lay that night at Orgon. We left late in the morning and arrived early. The commissioners would not allow one to take a single step without them.

"Before arriving at Auxerre we met in the plain the moving guillotine accompanied by a band of brigands dressed in the most horrible clothes. However, they did not say anything to us. They were going to Lyons.

"Having arrived at the Cour de France, the Prince alighted for dinner. While the repast was being prepared I noticed that the commissioners had written a letter in an alcove and had sent it off by a postillion. I immediately told the Prince about it, and His Highness thought that this letter had no other purpose than to announce his arrival. This turned out to be correct. We left for Paris as soon as dinner was finished. In passing through the rue Saint-Victor an individual stopped the coach and got in. It was le sieur Simonin, commissaire of the Conciergerie. He had the coach driven into the courtyard of the Palais du Justice, which we found full of curious onlookers. They did not say anything to us, and contented themselves with staring at us.

"The Prince alighted from the coach and was conducted into this horrible place, from where he only came out to go to his death. As for me, they did not want to let me out of their sight and put me in a little room next to the concierge."

After Philippe had been questioned by two prison officials Gamasche was allowed to go into his cell.

"As I came into the Prince's room His Highness said to me, 'It seems that they raised difficulties about letting you come in, my dear Gamasche. I would have been very sorry if we had been separated.' 'I also, citizen. I have done everything I could to join you and not to leave you.' 'Thank you, Gamasche. Let us hope that we won't always be in prison.'"

Gamasche wrote the following comment upon this conversation: "In spite of the repugnance which I experienced in pronouncing this word citizen, I was obliged to use it by force of circumstances."

Shortly after Gamasche had joined his master two gendarmes entered the cell and remained on guard.

"I was near the Prince, who said to me, 'Prison

spies that they are putting in our room.' The guards
were changed every two hours, night and day. The
room was small and we had our two truckle beds
which took up a lot of room.

"The Prince, who was tired out, asked about eight
o'clock for some vegetables for our supper. And we
went to bed, having two men walking back and forth
in the room all night. The next day Monseigneur
asked the caterer for what he wanted for his dinner.
It was brought at two o'clock, and after dinner, not
knowing what to do, we played a game of piquet.
Sometimes the concierge lent us some books, and
some of the guards, less strict than others, left us a
little freedom by withdrawing near the window.

"On Tuesday afternoon Monseigneur was told that
he would be questioned during the evening, and they
sent to fetch him at eight o'clock. He returned at
nine and went to bed, after having supper.

"The Prince was agitated all night, and he told
me when he got up that he wanted to breakfast early
because he had to appear before the tribunal. I had
some potatoes fried for him, which he was very fond
of. I was far from believing that it was the last meal
that I would ever prepare for him.

"At nine o'clock M. Voidel came to see Monseigneur (he was his legal defender). He was in the
best of humour, and believed the Prince was saved,
judging by what he said; but, unhappily, he was condemned before appearing before the tribunal."

Gamasche has left an interesting note to explain
this statement. He says that his wife had tried every

way possible to see him, but without success. Finally
she went to Fouquier-Tinville himself and asked him
what her husband's fate was to be. He asked her how
old she was. "Twenty-two," she replied. "At your
age, one husband lost, a hundred found." At this
grim pleasantry Gamasche's young wife burst into
tears. Fouquier-Tinville reflected a moment, took up
a pen and scribbled a note. "Listen," he said, "Orléans
will die on Wednesday, and I will do what I can to
give you back your husband."

"It is easy to see," remarks Gamasche, "that the
trial of the Prince was a mere formality, and that he
was condemned before arriving in Paris."

"At ten o'clock," the account continues, "the
officer of the gendarmes and the commissioner came
to get the Prince and invited him to leave his watch
and his pocket-book, saying that they might be stolen
passing through the crowd. (They themselves were
the robbers.) Monseigneur gave me these two objects,
looking fixedly at me. He was agitated; and as for
me, I was trembling."

That was the last that poor Gamasche saw of his
master. They shut him up in solitary confinement,
and he knew nothing more until all was over. Then
he was called before a prison committee and Philippe's
watch was taken away from him. They forgot to ask
for the pocket-book, and Gamasche kept it until long
after the Terror, when he restored it to Mlle Orléans
upon her return to France. All the rest of Philippe's
personal things were sold at the Palais Royal. As for
Gamasche, he returned to service with the House of

Orléans during the restoration, and in 1827, when he wrote his account of Philippe's last days, he was concierge of the garden at Monceau.

When Philippe left Gamasche he was taken at once before the dreaded tribunal to be questioned by Fouquier-Tinville. After he had given his name, Louis-Philippe-Joseph Égalité, his age, 46, his residence, Paris, the clerk of the court read out the charges and the "trial" began. Most of the questions were stupid. One or two, however, throw some light upon Philippe's relationships.

Fouquier-Tinville asked, "Since when did you cease being intimate with Pétion?"

"Since he advised me to give my resignation as representative of the people."

The Girondists were already dead, and among them had been Sillery. But Mme de Genlis had escaped to Switzerland with Mlle Orléans. Fouquier-Tinville declared her to be an intriguer and made it a crime for Philippe to have entrusted his daughter to her.

"Was not the reason of your daughter's journey to England to marry her to some prince of the English Royal House?" he asked.

"No."

"What were the motives of your pretended mission to England?"

"It was known that I was in close touch with the party of the opposition, and it was a question of promoting peace with England at that time."

The last question was equally silly when considered as a reason for the death sentence.

"What were the causes of the great largess that you have made during the Revolution?"

"I have not made any great largess at all. I was happy enough to be of some help to my fellow-citizens during a severe winter by selling a small portion of my properties."

At the end of the questions Voidel, as counsel for the defence, made an eloquent and vain appeal. The jury did not even retire, and the president of the court, after reading the charges of conspiracy against the unity and indivisibility of the Republic and the safety of the French people (the same charges which had murdered the Girondists), pronounced sentence of death.

"The Duke of Orléans," wrote Beaulieu, "who until then had not passed for a courageous man, showed, however, the greatest fortitude in his last moments. . . . He appeared at the moment of his trial to have found again the character that a Frenchman likes to find in a descendant of Henry IV."

Immediately after the trial he was led back to the Conciergerie, where the last strange scene took place.

A priest named the Abbé Lothringer had received a letter from Fouquier-Tinville authorising him to offer the prisoner the comforts of religion. He found Philippe willing to receive him and eager to make his confession. But there was a drunken man in the same room, condemned to death for having thrown bread into the latrines. He shrieked and blasphemed so that it seemed impossible to do anything. Suddenly the drunkard fell asleep.

"The Duke of Orléans," wrote the Abbé, "went down on his knees and asked me if there were time to make a general confession. I said, ' Yes,' and that no one had the right to interrupt him, and he made a general confession of his whole life. . . . 'I die innocent of what they accuse me,' he said. ' May God pardon them as I pardon them. I deserve death for the expiation of my sins. I have contributed to the death of an innocent man—and here is my death! But he was too good not to pardon me. God will join us both with St. Louis."

"I cannot express strongly enough," wrote the Abbé, "how much I was edified by his noble resignation."

But now the moment had come to start on the final journey. Philippe got up and went out of the cell into the courtyard, where the tumbril was waiting. Beaulieu, who was in prison at that moment, looking out of his cell window, saw him passing through the courtyard and the gates of the conciergerie. "He was accompanied by a dozen gendarmes who encircled him with drawn sabres, and I must say that from his fiery and assured appearance, his truly noble air, one would have taken him rather for a conqueror who was commanding his troops, than for a miserable wretch whom these gaolers were leading to the scaffold."

His companions on this last journey were M. Coustard of Nantes, a member of the Convention accused of federalism, a wretched mender of chairs named Lesage, and an old soldier of 73 named Laroque from Caen, the scene of Girondist activities. This old man, upon seeing Philippe enter the condemned cell, had cried out: ' I no longer regret my life now that he who has lost my country receives the punishment for his crimes; but what does humiliate me is to be obliged to die on the same scaffold with him.'

Philippe made no answer, nor did he appear to notice the jeers and insults that followed him along the route to the guillotine.

"Every one with any sense of impartiality who saw him on his way to death assured me," wrote Montjoie, "that on that day he was a man and a prince. His countenance was noble and assured, without the least affectation, his head was held high and rose above those of his companions, who seemed crushed by the weight of their misfortune." And people noticed that he spoke encouraging words to Coustard, " who was already half enveloped in the night of the Tomb " and did not reply to him, probably did not even hear him.

When the tumbril arrived in front of the Palais Royal it stopped for about ten minutes. Philippe gazed at his former home with an expression that was completely unmoved, though his lips were seen to move as though he were reading to himself the sign: "National Property," that was stuck up on the walls. After a moment he turned his back on it and awaited his executioner's pleasure.

As the tumbril crawled on towards the Place de la Revolution more and more people gathered along the route. Cries of "I vote for death!" and insults of every sort were hurled at him. He made no sign whatever that he even heard them. When the horrible form of the guillotine came into view his face, usually so red, turned deathly white, but he gave no other sign of emotion. The cart arrived at the foot of the scaffold. He called Lothringer to him, and once more received absolution. Then he mounted the platform with a firm step. Samson's assistant wanted to take off his boots.

"You can do that more easily to my dead body," he said. "Come—be quick."

The knife fell, and the head that was held up to the crowd had a mocking smile of indifference on its dead lips.

BIBLIOGRAPHICAL NOTE

T HE bibliographical sources can be divided into
three main sections. There is first of all the huge
mass of anti-Orléanist writing which loads Philippe
with so much hate and calumny that he sinks into a
wilderness of dreary abuse.

First among these works is the *Histoire de la Con-
juration de L. P. J. d'Orléans surnommé Égalité*, written
by the royalist Galart de Montjoie and published in
Paris, 1796, 3 vols. Montjoie was an eye-witness of
many of the events which he describes, but his account
is based on the conviction that Philippe was the master
spirit behind the Revolution.

Other writers who are violently anti-Orléanist
include: Gazean de Vautibault, who compiled seven
volumes of accusations against the House of Orléans
under the title of *Les Orléans au Tribunal de l'histoire*,
Paris, 1887-89.

Laurentie: *Histoire des ducs d'Orléans*, Paris, 1832,
4 vols.

Crétineau-Joly: *Histoire de Louis-Philippe*, Paris
1862-63, 2 vols.

Laurent de l'Ardèche: *La Maison d'Orléans devant
la légitimité et la démocratie*, Paris, 1861.

Ducoin: *Philippe d'Orléans Égalité*.

All of these works, with the exception of the small
volume by Ducoin, are incredibly dreary reading.

Their violence is monotonous and their *idée fixe* that the House of Orléans, and Philippe in particular, are responsible for all the evil in the world is, to say the least, wonderfully unconvincing. Ducoin is not so long-winded, but he was a passionate legitimist, and hence a violent anti-Orléanist.

Directly opposed to this point of view is a volume by Tournois, *Louis Philippe Joseph duc d'Orléans*, Paris, 1842, which goes to the other extreme, and makes Philippe a paragon of all the virtues and a model for people and princes to emulate. It is quite as dull as the anti-Orléanist tomes.

The second section includes the memoirs and diaries of the period, of which those of Mme de Genlis must necessarily rank among the most important. They were published in London, 1825-26. Grace Dalrymple Elliot's *Journal During the Terror* (London, 1910), and Dr. Edward Rigby's *Letters from France* (London, 1880), are interesting and entertaining. Other memoirs include those of Mme Vigée Lebrun, *Souvenirs*, 2 vols. (Paris, 1867). Mme Roland's *Mémoires* (Paris, 1869). Gouveneur Morris' *Diaries*, 2 vols. (London, 1889), an invaluable commentary on men, women and events of the time.

Of great general interest are the *Essais Historiques*, of Claude Beaulieu, 6 vols. (Paris, 1801-03), and the *Mémoires* of Ferrières, 2 vols. (Paris, 1889). Both these writers took part in the events they record. Ferrières was a deputy for the Nobles in the National Assembly. Beaulieu's sense of proportion and balanced judgment are remarkable. These two important works are healthy antidotes to the volumes of the anti-Orléanists.

The published report of the Court of the Châtelet on the affairs of October 5th to 6th, 1789 (Paris, 1790), is essential to any inquiry into this famous episode. Other mémoires include those of:

Bertrand de Moleville (2 vols., Paris, 1816).

Lafayette (4 vols., Paris, 1837).

Barère (4 vols., Paris, 1842-44).

Mallet du Pin (Paris, 1851).

Talleyrand (Paris).

Two further contemporary works to be noted are the *Appel au Tribunal de l'Opinion Publique* by J. J. Mounier (Paris, 1790), and Garat's short commentary *De la Conspiration d'Orléans* (tome XXV., Paris, 1797).

The third section includes more modern works. Those directly concerned with Philippe include:

L'Idylle d'un Gouverneur by Gaston Maugras (Paris, 1904).

Le Général Choderlos de Laclos by Dard (Paris, 1890), a work of great interest and profound erudition.

La Famille Orléans pendant la Révolution by du Boscq de Beaumont (Paris, 1913), which contains important letters.

La Jeunesse de Philippe-Egalité by Amédée Britsch (Paris, 1926), a scholarly and very detailed work.

Mme. de Genlis by Jean Harmand (Paris, 1912).

Les Fils de Philippe Egalité pendant la Terreur by Lenôtre (Paris, 1908), a delightful book containing the prison memoirs of the young duc de Montpensier.

The more general works consulted include Taine's

famous volumes on the Revolution (Paris, 1875);
Bainville's *Histoire de France* (Paris, 1926); Gaxotte's
Révolution (Paris, 1929); Madelin, *La Contre Révolution*
(Paris, 1935), and Webster's *Revolution* (London, 1921),
and *Secret Societies* (London, 1928). These last two
books are especially interesting. Mrs. Webster is a
violent anti-Orléanist, and besides being a persuasive
writer she has marshalled the results of her penetrating
researches with great authority. However, although
I read her with the greatest pleasure and instruction, I
cannot persuade myself that Philippe was the arch
villain that he is made out to be.

INDEX

INDEX

INDEX